The Adopter's Handbook on Education (Scotland)
GETTING THE BEST FOR YOUR CHILD

Alison Rennie Parkinson
and Eileen Fursland

coramBAAF
ADOPTION & FOSTERING ACADEMY

Published by
CoramBAAF Adoption and Fostering Academy
41 Brunswick Square
London WC1N 1AZ
www.corambaaf.org.uk

Coram Academy Limited, registered as a company limited by guarantee in England and Wales number 9697712, part of the Coram group, charity number 312278

© Alison Rennie Parkinson and Eileen Fursland, 2021

British Library Cataloguing in Publication Data
A catalogue record for this book is available from the British Library

ISBN 978 1 910039 96 0

Project management by Jo Francis, CoramBAAF
Designed and typeset by Helen Joubert Design
Printed in Great Britain by The Lavenham Press

Trade distribution by Turnaround Publisher Services, Unit 3, Olympia Trading Estate, Coburg Road, London N22 6TZ

All rights reserved. Apart from any fair dealing for the purposes of research or private study, or criticism or review, as permitted under the Copyright, Designs and Patents Act 1988, this publication may not be reproduced, stored in a retrieval system, or transmitted in any form or by any means, without the prior written permission of the publishers.

The moral right of the authors has been asserted in accordance with the Copyright, Designs and Patents Act 1988.

For the latest news on CoramBAAF titles and special offers, sign up to our free publications bulletin at https://corambaaf.org.uk/subscribe.

Contents

	Introduction	1
1	**Supporting adopted children in school: the context**	4
	Pressures on schools	5
	Child and Adolescent Mental Health Services (CAMHS)	6
	Adoption support	7
	Corporate parents	8
	Virtual schools	8
2	**How do early experiences affect children's ability to cope with school and readiness to learn?**	11
	The impact of trauma and attachment difficulties	11
	Understanding the effects of FASD	17
	Difficulty in diagnosis	20
	Responding to needs, whatever the underlying cause	21
3	**Approaches to supporting adopted children in school**	23
	Building safety, self-regulation, trust and attachment	23
	The GIRFEC framework	26
	The additional support for learning framework	26
	Evaluating attachment-awareness work	28
	Attachment figures and having a "key person"	30
	Feeling safe in the classroom	31
	Helping a child who is becoming dysregulated	32
	Recognising behaviour as "communication"	33
	Emotional awareness	35
	Sensory issues	36
	Encouraging friendships	41
	Recognising trauma triggers and sensitive issues in the curriculum	42
	Helping a child with executive functioning difficulties	44
	Celebrating success	45
	Attachment Ambassadors	46

4	**Choosing and starting a new primary school**	**49**
	When is the best time to start school?	49
	Delaying when your child starts primary school	49
	Starting school in a pre-adoptive placement	52
	Choosing a primary school	56
	Key questions for primary schools	57
	Education outwith mainstream school	64
5	**Working with your child's school and teachers**	**68**
	Interaction between home and school	68
	Education planning for adopted children	70
	Pupil Equity Fund	72
	Care Experienced Children and Young People's Fund	73
	Be proactive about communicating with the school	74
	How much should you tell the school about your child's circumstances before you adopted them?	75
	Managing trauma triggers and curriculum hotspots	76
	Groups for adoptive parents	77
	Supporting your child through transitions	77
	Separation anxiety	79
	When the school isn't getting it	80
	When others ask you and your child about adoption	81
	Homework	83
	Safeguarding for adopted children	84
6	**Rights, additional support needs, exclusion and alternative provision**	**89**
	Admissions	89
	Additional Support Needs (ASN)	90
	Disabled children	90
	Co-ordinated support plans	91
	Exclusion	96
	Alternatives to exclusion	97
	Alternative arrangements	100
	If you want to challenge your child's exclusion	101
	Moving your child to a new school: personal accounts	102
	Home education	107
	Flexi schooling	108

7	**Choosing and starting a new secondary school**	**110**
	Choosing a secondary school	110
	Key questions for starting a new secondary school	110
	Transition to secondary school	113
	What can help?	115
	Communicating with secondary school	118
	Home/school partnership	118
	Adolescence and the teenage years	121
	Coming to terms with adoption	122
	Social networking	126

Conclusion: how adopted young people feel in school	**133**
References	**136**
Useful resources	**139**
Appendix: The education system: the basics	**148**
Types of schools	148
Learning structure	150
Getting it Right for Every Child (GIRFEC)	151
Teaching in groups	152
Additional support needs (ASN)	153
Who's who in the education system?	154
Role of local authorities	155
Learning review and assessment	156
Checking progress	157
School policies	159
Attendance	159
School uniform and general appearance	160
Parental involvement	160
Glossary	**162**

Notes about the authors

Alison Rennie Parkinson has spent most of her professional life in adult education working for the Health and Safety Executive and lecturing in Further Education. She and her husband adopted twins in 2004 and it was navigating their varied and challenging(!) school education journeys that led her to join Adoption UK in Scotland as a Helpline Adviser in 2016, and then move into the role of Training Lead in 2020.

Eileen Fursland is a freelance writer specialising in issues affecting children and young people. She has written extensively for BAAF (now CoramBAAF) on a number of publications since 2002, as well as for a range of magazines and national newspapers and other organisations.

Eileen's publications for BAAF include the training course *Preparing to Adopt* (she wrote the first edition in 2002 with a working party from BAAF which devised the course, and the fourth edition, 2014, with Nicky Probert and Elaine Dibben); *Facing up to Facebook* (second edition, 2013); *Social Networking and Contact* (2010); *Foster Care and Social Networking* (2011); *Social Networking and You* (2011); and *Ten Top Tips on Supporting Education*, with Kate Cairns and Chris Stanway. In earlier collaborations with Kate Cairns, she co-wrote BAAF's training programmes: *Trauma and Recovery*; *Safer Caring*; *Building Identity*; and *Transitions and Endings*. Most recently she wrote three books in this series: *The Adopter's Handbook on Therapy* (2016), *Caring for a Child who has been Sexually Exploited* (2018), *The Foster Carer's Handbook on Education* (2020), and *The Adopter's Handbook on Education* (2018), the latter two acting as companion guides to this book.

Acknowledgements (from Alison Rennie Parkinson)

It has been an education and a privilege to adapt Eileen's excellent publication for use in Scotland. My grateful thanks to the parents and young people who have contributed their experiences, to my colleagues at Adoption UK for their support, and in particular to Paula Gilhooly, support for learning teacher and adoptive parent, and to Janine McCullough, Senior Education Officer with Education Scotland for reading and commenting on the draft.

Introduction

Children spend on average over 7,800 hours of their life at school in the course of their education (OECD, 2014). At its best, school can be a place where young people learn to become all that they can be; it can open the doors to discovery, inspiration and friendship, as well as providing a well-rounded education that equips each child with the knowledge and skills they need for life. But it can also be a struggle, especially for those in care or adopted, when schools too often fail to meet children's learning needs and school life can be an ordeal for them.

As a parent, clearly your attitude to your child's education will go a long way towards shaping their expectations and aspirations and helping them to do as well as they can. Encouraging them and supporting them, sitting by their side and listening to them read, cheering on the sidelines when they're playing for the school football or netball team, helping them with homework, celebrating with them when they have tried hard or done well – these are all ways in which you will show your adopted child that you love them, that they are worthy of your time and care, that you think they are great, and that you want to help them learn. It will be a revelation for a child who has never had this before.

The school's approach, of course, is key when it comes to supporting children and young people who have experienced neglect and abuse (and those damaged even before birth) and who have different needs than those of their peers. They need understanding and extra support – sometimes a little, sometimes a lot – in order to simply cope with the demands of being at school, let alone to learn effectively.

Many adoptive parents say that they do not feel their children are being supported sufficiently at school. If a child is not enjoying it and is struggling, this is a source of stress not only for them but also for their worried parents.

This handbook is for you. By suggesting some of the things you need to know or do to support your child's education, it aims to help them have the best possible experience at school.

Much of the information and advice in this guide is likely to apply to children's experiences of school across the four countries of the UK. However, their educational systems vary. This guide, adapted from the original publication

(Fursland, 2018), makes reference to the framework in Scotland, but much of the content will be useful throughout the UK.[1]

We begin with a look at the context – the current social and economic pressures on schools and Child and Adolescent Mental Health Services (CAMHS), the role of additional support for learning, the experience of adoptive families, but also the potential impact of measures such as TESSA (Therapeutic, Education and Support Services in Adoption) and the Care Experienced Children and Young People's Fund (CECYPF). There follows a brief explanation of how a legacy of early traumatic and difficult attachment experiences may affect children's ability to cope with school life and learning. We go on to look at approaches that schools and teachers are using to support children, and how you, as a parent, can work with your child's school to help teachers and others understand their needs, as well as what you might be able to do to help your child cope with the demands of school. There are tips and case studies to help you navigate the system, including managing transitions to primary and secondary schools, working with teachers and accessing additional support for learning, plus a list of organisations and resources where you can get further information and support. An Appendix provides some basic information about who's who in the education system and how it works.

The combination of positive experiences of education and school and a stable, loving home can turn a child's life around. In the words of Collette Isabel Bentley, adopted at 10 years old after troubled years in foster and residential homes:

> *Time and time again, my education was a vehicle through which my "parents" transmitted a crucial message: 'You are worthy of our love, care and expectations.' As a child who had been rejected and abused, humiliated and shamed, it was overwhelmingly invigorating to have an adult care enough to learn my French vocabulary with me…to have an adult buy me an appropriate PE kit so I wouldn't have to face humiliation at school.*

(Bentley, 2013, pp.51–52)

There is still much that needs to improve in the Scottish education system. Training teachers and having enough staff in schools depends on resources and schools are in a funding crisis. The services that should be supporting

---

[1] For more information about education in the other devolved countries, visit: www.gov.wales/education-skills (Wales) and www.deni.gov.uk (Northern Ireland).

adoptive families also struggle at a time when local authority budgets are under severe strain. But with their adoptive parents to advocate for them, and with growing understanding among teachers, we hope that more and more adopted children will get the support they need and find school a safe and nurturing place where they can achieve everything they are capable of. There are some encouraging developments. A growing number of adoption support organisations, parents and other individuals with expertise in this area are working to get schools and teachers to understand the issues and change their ethos, cultures and classroom practices, and promote positive relationships and behaviour. An increasing number of schools are finding out how to get it right for adopted children and other young people who have had adverse early experiences.

Every child is unique. Every school is different. We know that a book like this can never address every question and there are no easy answers to many of the issues around adopted children and schools. Hopefully you will find things that make you reflect, or that spark ideas you could share with your child's teachers. Above all, we hope that it will help you to support your child to be able to enjoy school life and make the most of everything it offers.

1 Supporting adopted children in school: the context

Children who have been adopted after a period of being in care (previously "looked after" in legal terminology) are now in a loving home with a parent or parents who will work hard to support their education. Many of them will make accelerated progress in school once they are settled, and go on to do very well. But it is recognised that some of these children are still likely to need extra help.

> *There is continuing evidence that educational outcomes for care experienced young people are poor in comparison to their non-care experienced peers. Trauma, mental ill health, stigma, frequent placement moves, and chaotic living arrangements are all examples of how a young person's experience of education can be affected by being in care.*

(Who Cares? Scotland, January 2018, p.1)

Adopted children gain the immediate benefits of stability and committed parenting but the legacy of their backgrounds and multiple adverse experiences is not quickly overcome. Many adoptive parents find themselves struggling to have the needs of their children recognised and attributed to their early experiences rather than their current parenting. Adoption UK (AUK) surveys confirm that education is a major concern for many adoptive families. In 2014, 75 per cent of adoptive parents said that their child's experience of neglect/abuse in early life had affected their schooling, and 80 per cent that their child needed more support (Adoption UK, 2014 (UK figures)). Four years later, 78 per cent of adopted children surveyed said that 'other children seem to enjoy school more than me', and 60 per cent of their parents that they felt their adopted child did not have an equal chance in school (Adoption UK, 2018 (Scottish figures)).

Pressures on schools

Even if it is recognised that many adopted children have additional needs in the classroom, teachers have a punishing workload and the demands on their time are huge. Most adoptive parents are only too well aware of the challenges teachers face in meeting the needs of all the children in their child's class, of whom one-third or more may have additional support needs (ASN) of one kind or another.

With austerity and the Covid-19 pandemic having affected school budgets and arrangements as never before, accessing extra help or one-to-one support for children who need it is not always easy. Many schools and colleges have been forced to review how they support pupils with ASN, which has resulted in some children and young people receiving less support than they had previously. A recent review of the implementation of additional support for learning legislation found that:

> ...there is a significant disconnect between experience and the stated aspirations of the legislation and policy...

(Scottish Government, 2020, p.15)

Local support services for children and families have been cut to the bone in many areas. This means that there are increasing demands on schools and teachers to deal with issues in families struggling with anything from debt to domestic abuse which might, in the past, have been dealt with by other agencies.

Academic achievement in schools is highly valued which, of course, it should be. The Scottish Government does not publish official school league tables but there are unofficial ones produced by newspapers which place pressure on head teachers and teachers, not to mention children and young people themselves. This should not exclude all other considerations, and definitely not if this means discouraging or even excluding children who are unable to reach the required standards.

> There is a different way: a way that not only provides an equal chance for children who have not had an equal start in life, but which can provide a foundation for excellence for every child that comes into our classrooms.

(Adoption UK, 2019, p.18)

Scotland's national curriculum, Curriculum for Excellence (CfE) (see Appendix) aims to provide inclusive education that meets the needs of all children. However, it is yet to move completely from being a prescribed curriculum to becoming an implemented curriculum with practices that truly reflect its core principles in every school.

Child and Adolescent Mental Health Services (CAMHS)

Children's and young people's mental health and the state of services for them are of huge concern to professionals, parents and children alike. The Scottish Government's Mental Health Strategy has a very simple and clear guiding ambition:

> *To prevent and treat mental health problems with the same commitment, passion and drive as ... physical health problems...*

and that:

> *...you should only have to ask once to get help fast.*

> Scottish Government (2017a, p.2)

The Children and Young People's Mental Health Task Force, commissioned by Scottish Government and the Convention of Scottish Local Authorities (COSLA) in 2018, emphasised the importance of a preventative, whole systems approach:

> *Many children and young people may need extra help at some point, and some could need additional or specialist support. This may be because of factors relating to the child's development or health profile or it could be because of the impact of adverse experiences on the child, family or community. If required, this help should be delivered in line with the Getting it Right for Every Child (GIRFEC) approach and "National Practice Model". Additional support should be provided promptly, wherever possible within universal services and the community, and should be proportionate to the level of need and risk. Where this is not possible there can be no "wrong door" for children and families who need to receive extra help – they should only have to ask once to access services. Wherever requested, for example through school or from a GP or Health Visitor, there should be a helpful*

and appropriate response – bureaucracy or organisational and professional boundaries should not get in the way.

(Scottish Government, 2019, p.4)

While it is reassuring to see that policies are setting a positive direction, the situation on the ground is often very difficult. Teachers can feel that they lack training and confidence in addressing their pupils' mental health concerns, and although increased emphasis on well-being is producing more resources, they may struggle to find the time to assimilate them. (See Education Scotland's National Improvement hub for resources: https://education.gov.scot/improvement/learning-resources/resources-for-school-staff-to-support-positive-mental-wellbeing-of-children-and-young-people/.)

CAMHS is notoriously overstretched. While the majority of patients are "seen" within the Scottish Government's target of 18 weeks, this is often followed by a long wait for proper investigation and support. In 2019, the number of children/teenagers waiting over a year for treatment increased compared to the previous year, and there is also an element of "postcode lottery". Adoptive parents struggle to get their children referred to CAMHS or, if referred, find the services available to be unsuitable.

Adoption support

In Scotland, there is no exact counterpart for the England Adoption Support Fund (ASF), which while not funding educational support directly, does provide a limited pot of money for therapeutic psychological support for adopted children and their families. In Scotland, children adopted from care may benefit from education support funded from the Attainment Scotland Fund, but identifying what is available and accessing it is not straightforward (see Chapter 5, 'Pupil Equity Fund' and 'Care Experienced Children and Young People's Fund'). For individual assistance, adoptive families have to contact their local authority and/or adoption agency or they may be eligible to access TESSA (see Useful resources (Adoption UK)).

Corporate parents

All state schools are "corporate parents" for looked after children.[1] This means that they have statutory duties to collaborate with other corporate parents (such as local authorities) in upholding the rights and securing the well-being of looked after children in the same way a good parent would. Children placed with adoptive parents but not yet legally adopted are still looked after children and their school should be aware of this. Looked after children are deemed to have additional support needs (ASN) unless the local authority determines that they do not require additional support to enable them to benefit from school.[2] Parents adopting a child who has already started school should investigate whether their child has already had an assessment for ASN or received support in school. At the current time, the presumption of ASN does not extend beyond the adoption order as once this is granted, the child will have a parent or parents who will advocate for their child's needs to be addressed. Unfortunately, this inadvertently supports the myth that once a child is adopted, they will no longer have any problems!

The term "care experienced" is often used in preference to "looked after", since it is seen as less pejorative by those who have been through the care system and it includes those who have been through the care system but who are no longer part of it. Children adopted from the care system fall within this definition – they are care experienced although no longer looked after. This is an important distinction that allows adopted children and young people to apply to the Care Experienced Children and Young People's Fund (CECYPF) and to the Student Awards Agency Scotland (SAAS) for a care experienced bursary rather than a student loan, and to receive special consideration for places and support at institutions of Further and Higher Education. This is a recognition that early adverse experiences have long-term effects.

Virtual schools

Some local authorities in Scotland have chosen to establish a Virtual School or a Care Experienced Team but these do not have specific statutory duties

---

1   Children and Young People (Scotland) Act 2014 (CYP Act)

2   Education (Additional Support for Learning) (Scotland) Act 2004, as amended 2009 (ASL Act)

as English virtual schools do. Until the launch of the CECYPF, there was only one Scottish virtual school, which was part of Aberdeen City Council. Since the fund's inception, 15 other local authorities have used it to establish a virtual head teacher and/or a virtual school. Since there is no statutory framework, they are all quite different in how they operate.

However, if you adopt a child from England, you may have access to some support from a virtual school there, as this case study illustrates:

> *Charlotte was placed from England. She had a personal education plan (PEP) already in place so her school could pick that up and work from it. She was also part of the virtual school system from her placing authority which meant that her school received £1,800 annually until she was officially adopted a year-and-a-half later. They used it to purchase resources for her (discussed at her child planning meeting (CPM)), although the whole class benefited. The virtual school called the school daily to check her attendance. CPMs were discontinued at the end of P1 as Charlotte appeared to be coping academically and socially.*
>
> *Once Charlotte was legally adopted during P2, the PEP was replaced by standard school planning, and the virtual school involvement and money stopped. It took some time and persistent asking from me before the CPM process started up again. I suspect school agreed because by this time they could see that Charlotte was struggling socially and academically, although education policy was also becoming ACE [adverse childhood experience] aware and schools were being encouraged to do more.*
>
> (Fiona, adoptive mother)

Key points

- It is a challenging time for schools, mental health services and anyone who is concerned about the life chances of children with educational and mental health difficulties. Parents need to get all the support they can for their child, stay strong, mobilise and campaign – if they have the time and energy – and advocate for their child's needs.

- There is no direct funding for support of adopted children in school or legal presumption that they have additional support needs. However, the ASL Act covers all children. If an adopted child needs additional support for their learning, then this legislation gives adoptive parents a legal right to ask for their child's learning needs to be assessed.

- Adopted children are eligible to access support and initiatives funded by the CECYPF. Some local authorities have used this fund to establish virtual schools and/or virtual head teachers.

2 How do early experiences affect children's ability to cope with school and readiness to learn?

The lives of adopted children, even when they are in a loving and caring adoptive family, continue to be profoundly affected by what happened to them early on. The neglect, abuse, chaotic environments and traumatic events that caused them to be removed from their birth families, and the grief and loss of disrupted attachments can shape the way in which they see themselves, other people and the world around them. Children who have had a difficult start can be left with vulnerabilities and gaps in terms of their psychological and social development and their ability to regulate their emotions and behaviours.

A child may be highly intelligent but unable to do well at school – or sometimes even cope with school at all – because of emotional, social and behavioural difficulties that are the legacy of their early experiences. It's worrying and distressing for parents to see that their child is stressed or unhappy in school, falling behind his peers or struggling to make friends because of his difficulties in forming relationships, or because his unpredictable behaviour makes other children wary of him.

For some adopted children, the womb was not a safe place. They may have been exposed to alcohol, drugs or stress hormones even before their mother knew she was pregnant. The effects of these, particularly alcohol, can be lifelong (see 'Understanding the effects of FASD' later in this chapter).

The impact of trauma and attachment difficulties

We know that many adopted children did not get the warm, responsive, attuned parenting that builds secure attachments between babies and their parents or carers. When children are neglected and abused by their main caregiver(s), this affects their ability to form secure attachments. These early experiences can have a long-lasting impact on many aspects of a child's later development, including learning, emotions and social skills. For example, they may struggle to understand, express and control their emotions and may often feel unsafe, under stress or overwhelmed by feelings of shame even when they are in a loving adoptive family:

> *Due to earlier trauma and disrupted attachment experiences and negative internal working models, children will often see themselves, others and their world through their trauma and insecure attachment mirror... 'I'm vulnerable', 'Others are dangerous', and 'The world is unsafe'. Therefore, although they may currently be in a "safe" school environment, this does not mean that they feel and believe that they are safe...and so we often see children's strongly developed defences/fight-flight-freeze at play within the school context.*
>
> (Treisman, 2017, p.149)

Repeated losses – being removed from the birth family home, being moved from foster carers – can leave them with unresolved grief and the constant fear that they will once again be taken away from everything they know. All adopted children will have experienced at least one disrupted or broken attachment. As a consequence, many develop an insecure attachment style: they relate to others in an anxious, avoidant, angry/ambivalent or disorganised way. They find it difficult to put their trust in adults, seek comfort, accept guidance, feel safe, make friends, empathise with others and to achieve many of the everyday things that come easily to other children.

Children cannot learn if they feel unsafe, if they cannot trust their teacher or if they are too afraid of rejection and failure to try and learn new things.

Building a new attachment with a child who is placed with you for adoption can take a long time. And at school, your child has to spend long periods of time away from you and share the teacher's attention with many other children. This can trigger his attachment needs or attachment-related trauma, as he wonders whether Mum/Dad will still be there when he gets home and whether they will have forgotten him.

Teachers are increasingly becoming aware of the importance of attachment, and children who used to be seen as "clingy, attention-seeking and disruptive" are now being recognised as "attachment-seeking".

Here are two short case studies showing how attachment difficulties can play out in the classroom:

> *Ten-year-old Amber...would regularly shout out in class and often follow the teacher around the room. Through a thorough assessment, it emerged that Amber had previously been starved of adult attention, and had been significantly neglected. She had learned various survival strategies for being kept in the minds of others; her shouting out was her way of communicating, 'Don't forget me, please remember me'.*
>
> *Five-year-old Dylan had experienced unavailable/absent parenting. He had learned to conceal, internalise and/or deny his emotions. Within the classroom this showed itself as Dylan being overly self-reliant and compliant. He avoided teacher support, seemingly from fear of being rejected or ignored. This, in turn, made him fall under the radar and appear "invisible", and once again mirrored his early experiences of being forgotten and neglected. This reinforced Dylan's insecure–avoidant attachment style and his expectations of being ignored, invisible and unimportant.*

(Treisman, 2017, p.148)

School requires children to trust adults and relinquish control to them – something that children who have experienced abuse at the hands of trusted adults can find particularly difficult to do. This can go against the defence mechanisms and "survival strategies" they may have developed in their birth families.

Children's difficulties also affect their relationships with other children. Sometimes their emotional and behavioural needs can make it hard for them to make and keep friends. If a child is withdrawn, or too controlling, is volatile and prone to lashing out or having meltdowns, has not learned to take turns and share, other children will be wary of them.

Feeling unsafe

The feeling of lack of safety described earlier can result in children becoming "hypervigilant" or "dissociating" at times of stress. When they feel unsafe (which may be much of the time while they are at school), children can be on high alert, constantly in "fight" mode and preoccupied with possible threats. This means that they may overreact to things such as someone touching them or appearing suddenly behind them, which can mean they "kick off" in the classroom and, if the teacher doesn't understand, can find themselves in trouble. The playground can be particularly difficult as the safety provided by supervision is less obvious and the perceived "threat" from unpredictability, volume of stimulation and massive sensory overload, enormous.

In other children, or at other times, the child "zones out", withdraws and becomes dissociated from everything going on around them. The teacher may interpret this as simply not paying attention, daydreaming, and so on.

Such children may even do certain things without realising consciously what they are doing, which again can get them into trouble.

Dysregulation

If babies have not been cared for by an adult who is attuned to their emotions, who is there to soothe them and help them calm when they are distressed, they will not develop the ability to reliably regulate their own emotions. They can quickly become overwhelmed by feelings of stress and fear (which may play out as anger).

Dysregulated behaviour can look different for every child. In the classroom it might mean fidgeting, making repetitive noises, calling out, chattering and giggling, lashing out, becoming withdrawn and even things like urinating somewhere inappropriate. A dysregulated child is liable to flare up, over-react to seemingly small things, or become overwhelmed in stressful situations. These behaviours, of course, often don't go down well in the classroom or with peers. Their impulsive, volatile behaviour can get them into trouble.

Dysregulated children need an adult to whom they are attached who can help them to regulate their emotions when they are feeling stressed, angry or upset. With help, as they grow older, children can develop some understanding of why they may struggle with their feelings and emotions. This 12-year-old adopted child describes it like this (with their own unique spellings!):

> *My brain works differently to other children and some of your sons' or daughters' brains will work the same as mine. So some of your children mite not no they need to think about other people feeling but children who haven't had so much trauma in there life will no you need to think about other people's feelings as well as theirs. Some of your children will always*

think you are telling them off if you are saying 'Please don't do that'. But they are not doing it to make your life hard, they think you are telling them off. Maybe some of your children when you are about to say something think you are going to tell them off even if you were going to tell them something nice. Lots of adopted children brains work like that so if they are shouting at you, are screaming or hitting or kicking, you still have to deal with it but never take it personally, they aren't doing it because they hate you, they are doing it because they are angry. But half way through that meltdown they are sorry but they feel bad or embarrassed so they don't know how they say that so they try to get you drawn in so then they can say, 'But you did this,' so then this isn't on them. So the top tip in all of this is never take it personally.

(Anonymous, 2017)

Chronological age vs developmental age

Delays in children's development can mean that they feel, think and act much younger than they are. In school, adopted children often suffer because people's expectations are based on their chronological rather than their developmental age – and some are still operating at the emotional age of a toddler or much younger child:

They are often not developmentally mature enough to manage the requirements for independent goal-directed behaviours, impulse control, delay of gratification, anticipation of consequences and anticipation of their thoughts and feelings.

(Hughes, 2012, p.37)

These children need teachers who understand this and can provide appropriate learning and play activities, supervision, boundaries and targets.

Executive functioning difficulties

Many adopted children experience difficulties with "executive functioning", namely the ability to organise, concentrate, set goals, plan tasks, process information, solve problems, switch focus from one task to another, and remember information and instructions. Problems with executive functioning can also make it more difficult for children to anticipate the consequences of their actions. It's easy to see how this makes school life and learning challenging for children. They may forget to bring into school the things they need, or have trouble concentrating or switching from one task to another, or find it hard to finish work in the time allowed.

Sensory issues and triggers

Developmental trauma affects the ability to process and integrate the information received from the senses – sights, sound, smell, touch, taste, body awareness and balance. Children may be unable to recognise when they are too cold, too warm, hungry or thirsty. Some are over-sensitive to sensory input and experience sensory overload in busy, bright and noisy classrooms. Certain smells and tastes can seem overpowering to them. Even their clothes may feel scratchy and uncomfortable.

When a child has sensory issues, the clamour of the classroom, crowds of children in the corridor, shouting in the playground and the queue in the dining hall can leave him feeling too stressed to function or even, sometimes, unwilling to go to school at all.

Negative expectations

The child may have spent his early years in a family where adults failed to attune to or meet his needs or even left him isolated and rejected, which will have shaped his view of himself, others and the world around him. He may have internalised the notion of adults as intrinsically uncaring or hurtful, of the world as an unsafe place and of himself as a "bad child" who is worthless and deserves to be hurt. He may make negative assumptions about other people's motives.

In school, he may always expect to get things wrong, or to fail and may experience any mild form of instruction or correction as being told off or shouted at. He may expect rejection everywhere and believe that none of the other children like him, even if this isn't true.

In some cases, older children may also have absorbed the views of their birth parents that school is a waste of time, teachers are stupid, and there is no point in learning.

> *If we think we're in trouble it's going to make the situation a whole lot worse than it originally was...and then we just think it's going to happen all*

> over again – we're going to be kicked out of school or something like that, because we always think we're at fault.
>
> (Adopted young person speaking on a film produced by Coram Life Education)

Understanding the effects of FASD

> *The term Fetal* [sometimes spelt Foetal] *Alcohol Spectrum Disorder (FASD) describes a range of physical, emotional and developmental difficulties that may affect a person when they were exposed to alcohol during pregnancy.*
>
> (NHS Ayrshire & Arran, 2019, p.7)

FASD has begun to be recognised in the UK as a neurological/neurodevelopmental condition only relatively recently. It can affect the brain and nervous system, body systems and organs and is called a spectrum disorder because individuals are affected differently. FASD is often not detected at birth but can become apparent later in life, with a wide range of implications. Individuals may have difficulties with learning, social development and emotional regulation, but with early diagnosis and intervention, and the right supports, individuals can succeed in all areas of life.

There are commonalities and co-morbidity (conditions occurring together) with autism and attention deficit hyperactivity disorder (ADHD), and some individuals may be misdiagnosed with these conditions when FASD is the primary condition. Similar behaviours may occur in all these conditions and also as a result of developmental trauma and disrupted attachment, but the underlying causes are different. Unfortunately, adopted children with FASD are likely to be affected by developmental trauma and disrupted attachment as well, which is a further complication as they affect the brain in different ways to alcohol.

Scotland is the only country in the UK to have a recognised diagnostic pathway for FASD (since summer 2017), and awareness of the condition is improving. However, there is still a significant lack of understanding by professionals of the importance of recording evidence of women's alcohol consumption whilst pregnant. For example, social workers may record 'maternal substance abuse' in a child's record without identifying whether this refers to drugs or alcohol or both; medical staff may not record that a woman appeared drunk at a prenatal appointment. A diagnosis of FASD cannot be given without written evidence of prenatal alcohol exposure (PAE). Thus, many adoptive parents may not be aware, or may only have anecdotal evidence, that their child was exposed to alcohol in the womb, and may find it difficult to obtain this information retrospectively.

Supporting a child with FASD in school can be challenging because the condition is so variable. It is common for children with FASD to have a "spiky profile" in their developmental compared with their chronological age. For example, someone with FASD at physical age 18 years may have:

- the expressive language of a 20-year-old;
- the reading ability of a 16-year-old;
- the living skills of an 11-year-old;
- the money and time concepts of an 8-year-old;
- the social skills of a 7-year-old; and
- the comprehension and social maturity of a 6-year-old.

So they may really struggle with social skills and conceptual thinking but speak fluently using a good vocabulary, although their understanding may not match their spoken ability (expressive vs receptive language skills).

Difficulties may not become apparent until the child starts school or even later. Sometimes they do reasonably well in the nurturing and relatively controlled environment of primary school, but find the complex demands of secondary school more challenging. The Fetal Alcohol Advisory and Support Team (FAAST) (see Useful resources) has an excellent downloadable guide to help teachers to support learners affected by FASD in school, called *Understanding Fetal Alcohol Spectrum Disorder (FASD): What educators need to know*. (See www.nhsaaa.net/services-a-to-z/fetal-alcohol-spectrum-disorder-fasd.)

The resource is structured around the brain functions potentially affected by PAE, explaining each function, identifying the commonly associated child behaviours, and suggesting appropriate interventions and strategies that can be used. Examples of how these brain functions can impact at school include:

- **Executive functioning** – often repeating mistakes, difficulty understanding consequences. Rewards and sanctions systems don't work.

How do early experiences affect children's ability to cope with school and readiness to learn?

- **Sensory and motor** – over-react to sensory inputs such as noise. Might not be able to tolerate normal levels of noise in the classroom and become dysregulated or distressed.
- **Academic skills** – may possess normal IQ but need more practice to learn basic tasks and to make tasks automatic. Need to be provided with opportunities for this "over-learning".
- **Brain structure** – head circumference may be small. Can be difficult to find helmets that fit for activities on school trips.
- **Living and social skills** – may be socially vulnerable and easily taken advantage of. Classmates "set them up" to cause an incident and take the blame.
- **Focus and attention** – easily distracted or over-stimulated. May find it very hard to sit still.
- **Cognition** – difficulty with reasoning and thinking. It may take them longer to process information – "10-second children in a one-second world".
- **Communication** – may speak well but not always understand the full meaning of what's said. May be able to repeat instructions but not follow them.
- **Memory** – difficulty with short- and long-term memory. May seem forgetful. Sometimes appear to lie but are actually "filling in the blanks".
- **Affect regulation** – ability to manage emotions. May have difficulty coping well with emotions, easily aroused, very intense emotional reactions.

    Individuals with FASD need support throughout their lives. During the school years, those around them need to adjust their expectations and the environment to meet the needs of the individual rather than expecting the individual to adjust.

    (Aliy Brown, FASD Project Manager – FASD Hub Scotland (see Useful resources), personal communication)

It's important, as with all children, to see their strengths as well as their challenges. Identifying their strengths and building on them improves children's self-esteem and helps them to be successful in their learning. They should be praised, even for small achievements – they have often worked very hard for them. It is important that family, friends and professionals work together as a team. Children will learn best with consistency in language, routine, rules and expectations.

Difficulty in diagnosis

It may not be possible, or at least not early on, to get a firm diagnosis to explain the cause of a child's particular difficulties. The symptoms of many conditions can look a lot like each other with traits of multiple conditions and complex needs, but insufficient indicators for any particular diagnosis. It is not always straightforward.

To add to the difficulty, to get a diagnosis of a condition, the assessment may need to be carried out by a particular specialist – for example, a paediatrician for ADHD, an occupational therapist or sensory integration expert for sensory integration disorders, a speech and language therapist for communication problems, or an educational psychologist for other issues such as executive functioning problems and specific learning difficulties such as dyslexia and dyspraxia.

Getting your child's needs recognised, diagnosed and agreed by the various professionals and panels can be a long and challenging process. Some parents, faced with a long wait, resort to paying privately to have assessments done.

Traumatic stress in childhood seems to be linked to conditions like depression, anxiety, ADHD and conduct (behaviour) disorders. Children can also be subject to a range of other difficulties such as developmental delay, learning difficulty, speech and language issues and specific learning difficulties.

Some children show particularly extreme oppositional behaviour, which has been labelled "pathological demand avoidance" (PDA) – though some experts (and parents) are reluctant to apply diagnostic labels to children because of behaviour. These children will go to any lengths to refuse to co-operate with adults and other children. They use a range of behaviours to avoid complying, ranging from passivity and refusing to speak, to manipulative behaviour and "kicking off" in public.

It's been suggested that PDA could be a type of autism, but researchers are still not certain whether it is caused by some other disorder or is simply a separate entity that is often accompanied by other conditions. It's also not uncommon in children with language disorder and ADHD. Intervention and treatment are a challenge and currently largely a question of trial and error. Strategies developed for other conditions such as autism spectrum disorder (ASD) and ADHD are often ineffective. Obviously it is extremely difficult for a child or young person with these difficulties to function in a mainstream school classroom.

Responding to needs, whatever the underlying cause

The child's intrauterine environment (if the child was exposed to alcohol or drugs in the womb), genetic influences, early attachment experiences and adverse experiences in childhood all affect and contribute to the way they function and to the expression of conditions such as sensory processing difficulties, ADHD, FASD and depression. For example, children with attachment difficulties as well as those with FASD may be anxious about change and find it destabilising; become stressed and overwhelmed by aspects of school life; and find it less easy than their peers to form friendships with other children.

Gaining a diagnosis for any condition, especially those that affect a child's perception of the world around them and their education, can be the key that unlocks the door to greater understanding, gaining appropriate supports and development of skills to overcome their challenges. Ideally, every child would have a neurodevelopmental assessment that would identify their areas of strength and challenge. However, it is more likely that assessments will be undertaken to look for individual conditions, meaning that over time an individual may be assessed for more than one condition and gain multiple diagnoses. With this comes the risk of missing or not formally recognising areas of difficulty. A diagnosis can be helpful because it may well make it easier for everyone around the child to understand why he has these particular difficulties or behaves as he does. Hopefully it should also encourage teachers to have different expectations of the child and take the appropriate approach. With or without a formal diagnosis, the school is obligated to provide support for the learning needs the child has, regardless of the cause.

In more complex cases of ASN and disability, a child who meets the criteria may have a Co-ordinated Support Plan (CSP) set up for them which outlines the extra support they should receive (see Chapter 6).

In the following section, we look at some of the strategies that can help children feel safe, secure and calm, whatever the underlying causes of their difficulties. We explore the ways in which schools and teachers can make the school ethos and culture, classroom environment, teaching methods and even some curriculum topics more sensitive to the needs of adopted children.

One size doesn't fit all. The teacher needs to be able to get to know each individual child and be flexible and willing to adapt.

Key points

- Children's early experiences can have an enormous impact on their development, including their ability and readiness to learn. Teachers are beginning to understand this, in particular the role that attachment plays in how children cope with expressing and controlling their emotions, but there is still a long way to go.

- As an adoptive parent, you know your child best, so you will need to guide teachers about how best to help him feel safe and understood in the classroom.

- Children with early experiences of neglect or other abuse may feel, think and act much younger than they are. It is important that the school's expectations don't exceed your child's stage of development.

- Your child may have problems with "executive functioning", i.e. the ability to organise. Again, this needs to be recognised and understood.

- Many adopted children are likely to have been impacted by some level of prenatal alcohol exposure (PAE). Some will obtain an FASD diagnosis, others will not, but the effects can still be significant. Gaining an FASD diagnosis isn't easy, but there are a growing number of resources to help you identify whether this might apply to your child and, if so, what it can mean (see Useful resources, and the 'Further reading' section within it, at the end of this book).

3 Approaches to supporting adopted children in school

The context described in the opening chapter about the difficulties adopted children can have in school is obviously concerning to teachers and parents alike, but there is a great deal of positive work going on in schools across the country. This chapter looks at some of the approaches and strategies that schools and teachers are starting to use to help "tune in" to children and support them.

As stated earlier, you will have already gained considerable knowledge about trauma and attachment through your adoption preparation, training and reading, as well as knowing your own child better than anyone else. You will need to draw on this knowledge when it comes to talking with staff at your child's school and trying to raise awareness, or when you are visiting prospective schools if your child is approaching school age, or if you are thinking about changing school. (Chapter 5 goes into more detail about this.)

It's important to say that many adopted children don't necessarily need any special treatment or adjustments at school. They just get on with school, enjoy it and do well. But if schools can implement the approaches and strategies outlined here, there are benefits for all children, not only for those who face bigger challenges than their peers.

Building safety, self-regulation, trust and attachment

For children with developmental and relational trauma, feeling safe (at home and school) and developing attachment relationships (with their adoptive parents initially and then with teachers/school staff) are key to them feeling safe and able to learn in school. Of course, some children will also need treatment from therapists working together with you as the child's adopters in order to improve their emotional stability and achieve healthier attachments.

Many adoptive parents use the therapeutic parenting technique known as PLACE (playfulness, love, acceptance, curiosity and empathy), which aims to help the child feel safe and connected and to build stronger attachments. Professionals may use PACE or replace the "L" with "like" as being more appropriate than love. (For more information, see www.ddpnetwork.org/about-ddp/meant-pace.)

This is part of a parenting model called Dyadic Developmental Parenting (DDP), which is taught in a type of family-based psychotherapy or in group workshops. DDP was developed by Dan Hughes, who set up the Dyadic Developmental Psychotherapy Institute in the US. (For more information, see www.ddpnetwork.org/parents-carers.)

For a child to thrive in school, teachers as well as parents need to be able to behave in ways that will help the child feel safe and secure. "Playfulness" in a teacher can take the form of sharing fun and laughter in the classroom; "like" is about maintaining a positive attitude towards children who are not always easy to like; "acceptance" can mean accepting that the child's sometimes odd or challenging behaviours are not always under her conscious control. "Curiosity" means being interested in what makes the child tick – and perhaps wondering aloud: 'I'm wondering if this noise is bothering you?', or 'I'm guessing you are feeling upset because Mrs McLean is not here today?'. "Empathy" means really trying to connect with the child and understand how it might feel to find everyday situations threatening and live in a constant state of stress.

Dr Bruce Perry, senior fellow of the Child Trauma Academy in the US, researches, writes and lectures about neuroscience and trauma, particularly how childhood trauma and neglect affect the brain's stress response systems. He developed the Neurosequential Model of Therapeutics (NMT), a theoretical framework for looking at how trauma influences development. He argues that in some children the lower brain, where intense emotions originate, needs to be regulated with the help of an adult. Once the child is feeling calmer, the adult can relate to the child emotionally; then the adult can help her to reason, i.e. to understand why she might have done what she did or how she might have done things differently.

Emotional regulation and dysregulation (its opposite) are terms that are now much more commonly used in education and psychology as well as within the adoption community.

Bruce Perry suggests that patterned, repetitive and rhythmic somatosensory[1] activities such as music, dance, drumming, swinging and bouncing on a trampoline are good ways of reaching the dysregulated neural networks involved in the stress response. This knowledge and approach can be useful for teachers working with children who easily become dysregulated, as well as for parents.

Attempting to reason with or correct a child while she is in a highly aroused state of anger or distress will not work. What she needs is for an adult to first help her calm down and connect with her.

"Co-regulating" by an adult can eventually lead to the child developing the ability to self-regulate. They need to learn to recognise and identify her feelings and find ways to de-escalate when becoming stressed or angry.

Bruce Perry went on to develop the Neurosequential Model in Education, to look at how NMT can be applied in a classroom setting by school staff who have been taught what makes an optimal learning environment for a child with a history of trauma.

How does this work in practice? It's still early days for this approach, but in 2016, in a small-scale qualitative study of four teachers using NME in Canada, it was found that:

> *The NME model increased teacher, educational assistant and student knowledge about the brain, brain development and the impact trauma has on the brain, and provided tools to help with student self-regulation, preparing the classroom atmosphere for improved learning.*
>
> (Walter, 2016)

Some of the tools used were "brain/regulation breaks"; making a "mini-map" of the functioning of a child (looking at things like reactivity/impulsivity, self-regulation and attention/distractibility); heart-rate monitors to help students build awareness of their heart rate during difficult situations; and having students write a journal every day to reflect on what made them worry, what made them upset, and what made them feel better, to help them become more aware of their feelings and triggers and how to cope.

---

[1] Relating to a sensation that can occur anywhere in the body.

> *Participants used the NME classroom management tool "Regulate>Relate>Reason" to respond to student challenges by providing regulatory opportunities first, then relating to the student, and finally reasoning with the student.*
>
> (Walter, 2016)

There is no one single therapeutic technique or practice that will address all the complex needs of traumatised children at all stages of their development. But thanks to experts like Dan Hughes, Bruce Perry and others who are writing and providing training in the UK, together with the work of organisations such as Adoption UK (AUK), Scottish Attachment in Action (SAIA), Children in Scotland, and Centre for Excellence for Children's Care and Protection in Scotland (CELCIS), among others, there is a growing body of knowledge about approaches and strategies that parents and teachers find helpful.

The GIRFEC framework

In Scotland, the overall framework for young people is designed to be holistic, with their well-being and rights at its centre. The national approach, called 'Getting It Right For Every Child' (GIRFEC) is supposed to:

> *...provide a framework within which services offer the right help, at the right time, from the right people*
>
> (Scottish Government, 2017b, p.2)

This aims to ensure that all organisations that work for and with children and their families (not just schools) provide a consistent, supportive approach for all children. Parts of GIRFEC related to planning (for every child) and a child's plan (for those who require more cross-agency support) are legal requirements under the CYP Act.

The additional support for learning framework

This framework was introduced through the ASL Act. Children may have additional support needs (ASN) if:

...they are unable to benefit from their school education without the kind of help that is normally given to children and young people of their age.

(Enquire, 2019, p.6)

Many adopted children have an emotional and developmental age that is lower than their chronological age, as well as other issues that cause them to have difficulties at school, and so will need support in school and possibly also to help them prepare for school entry, or even for nursery. It is important to identify ASN as early as possible so that appropriate support can be put in place. This can prevent further difficulties at a later stage and maximise the child's ability to learn. Not all adopted children will have ASN, but problems with school are the most common reason why adoptive parents call the Adoption UK in Scotland Helpline, and are a consistent theme in online forums. So it is sensible to be prepared and to act on any concerns you may have, especially if your child has been with you for some time before they start school. Parents have a right to ask their local authority (generally, but not necessarily, in partnership with their pre-school centre or school) to arrange an assessment to see if their child has ASN. If your child started school as a looked after child before they were placed with you, try and get as much information from their previous school as possible, particularly if any assessments were done, any concerns noted, or any support plans put in place. Further information can be found in the statutory guidance,[1] Enquire's *Parents' Guide* (see Useful resources) and Factsheet, *Identifying and Assessing your Child's Needs* (www.enquire.org.uk/publications/identifying-assessing).

In recent years, there has been much more acceptance in Scottish education of the importance of well-being and relationship-based approaches to support children and young people, and there is increasing understanding of attachment theory, the effect on children of adverse childhood experiences (ACEs), and trauma (Education Scotland, 2018). Simply put, if children are stressed, they cannot learn – so supporting them to feel safe and nurtured helps remove barriers to their learning, raises achievement across the school and makes children feel happier.

The message is getting through that "difficult" or "challenging" behaviours that some children show in the classroom or playground are an expression of

---

[1] *The Supporting Children's Learning Code of Practice* (3rd edition). Statutory Guidance for the Education (Additional Support for Learning) (Scotland) Act 2004 (as amended).

their feelings of stress, fear, anxiety and being overwhelmed by emotions that they cannot control. There is a growing realisation that traditional sanctions and methods of managing behaviour in the classroom may not work with traumatised children, and an increasing readiness to adapt to their individual needs.

Many teachers are becoming more aware of things that might trigger anxiety, panic, overwhelming emotions or distressing memories in an adopted child; they are becoming more thoughtful about the curriculum topics that might make a child feel "different" or singled out because they are adopted. This is thanks to the work of many individuals, organisations and institutions – and, crucially, adopted children and young people and their parents.

Thus, initiatives such as nurture groups, attachment ambassadors and trauma-informed practice have provided training, support and recognition for schools that are doing the right things. With whole-school training and sometimes consultation with experts, school staff can come to understand the underlying reasons for children's behaviour; to recognise that tried and tested teaching methods and behaviour management systems may have limited or no success with children who have trauma-related and attachment difficulties or FASD; and to adopt a different approach that promotes feelings of safety and emphasises nurturing and relationships. In these schools, head teachers, teachers and other school staff are making adjustments in their schools, classrooms, teaching styles and pastoral support systems in order to help mitigate the challenges that school life can pose for adopted children.

(For details of experts, support organisations, training and information, see Useful resources.)

Evaluating attachment-awareness work

Many people are convinced that all this work is having good results. In 2012, CELCIS and SAIA carried out a mapping exercise of attachment-informed practice across all children's services (Furnivall *et al*, 2012), and described how Glasgow City Council had invested heavily in providing nurture groups, often based on attachment theory, in many of its primary schools and some early years provision. Benefits were noted in school and at home, where parents described their children as "transformed". Another initiative was the provision of volunteer counsellors in Edinburgh and Glasgow primary schools through the Place2Be organisation. Their training was strongly based on attachment theory and helped to transform the understanding and management of children's behaviour. The counselling was easily accessible to children individually and in groups, and also available to teachers and parents. This service was quickly felt to be indispensable in those schools that had access to Place2Be. Adoption UK in Scotland ran an 18-month project with an East Lothian primary and high school cluster aimed at reducing the attainment gap by helping children with attachment difficulties cope better at school. Training and workshops were provided for school staff and parents, and "Attachment Ambassadors" were nominated in each school. A key part of the project was collaborative working between the schools and the building of relationships between parents, children and school.

The project was well received and indicated that there was a need for this kind of input. Teachers provided the following feedback:

> *It was a bit of an unknown – wasn't sure what to expect. It's been a really worthwhile thing to do – I can see how and when I can apply it. The Nurture Room has come off the back of it...*

> *Calmer, less anxious pupils, more ready to learn, less unregulated and violent behaviour.*

> *We need this! It really does need to be rolled out. Some schools have children in every class with attachment issues!*

> (Project summary available at: www.celcis.org/knowledge-bank/search-bank/blog/2017/05/relationships-are-everything)

South Lanarkshire Council developed an attachment strategy as part of their Children's Services Plan (South Lanarkshire Council 2017–20), which promoted attachment-informed practice from early years to secondary aged children and young people, and informed training plans for the education workforce. They are also carrying out a programme of research to investigate how attachment-informed practice can be promoted and integrated into education policies and procedures, and the impact it will have on children.

Attachment figures and having a "key person"

Building trust and attachment can be difficult for class teachers when they do not have much time with the child every day and they have limited time to give one-to-one attention. Nonetheless, it is important for a child to have the opportunity to build attachment with one or two "safe" adults in school: this may be the teacher or Pupil Support Assistant (PSA), or someone else such as a member of the administration or catering team, librarian or janitor with whom the child has formed a relationship, who acts as a mentor and attachment figure.

As explained above, one of the key things an attachment figure can do is what Dan Hughes calls "connection before correction". In other words, this means connecting emotionally with the child, acknowledging their feelings and showing that you empathise with them before you attempt to model the desired behaviour.

Some schools identify a key member of staff for a child who has difficulties regulating their emotions, such as a PSA (see 'Helping a child who is becoming dysregulated', page 32).

Together with the child, the school identifies a person in school who is well placed to regulate that child and how they will do it. That person is sent for if the child is, for instance, having an angry outburst or a panic attack in the classroom. The key person will ideally get to know and understand the child well, build trust, anticipate the child's needs and difficulties, and advocate for the child within the school. In time, they may be able to help the child develop her reflective skills, emotional literacy and social skills.

Children can see their key person every morning when they arrive at school, or at breaktime or at the end of the school day, so they can discuss anything that is making them worried, upset or angry. The key person is someone who will provide one-to-one attention, listen and care when things are not going well, celebrate when things do go well, and acknowledge the challenges for the child. They may, for example, play turn-taking or trust games, or there might be a "bucket" where the child can metaphorically put people or things she doesn't like or is worried about.

Here's an example:

> *Seven-year-old Dante regularly had outbursts in both the classroom and at lunchtime. Through a process of really getting alongside Dante...and*

together with the support of attachment-informed consultation sessions, his teaching assistant was able to find several strategies that were effective in reducing incidents and increasing positive moments. Some of these included: having a personalised sensory box; starting the morning with drumming sessions; having a zen-zone filled with items such as weighted blankets and bubbles; using picture checklists; and having outdoor brain breaks.

(Treisman, 2017, p.156)

Feeling safe in the classroom

The following considerations are important when helping a child who is experiencing stress, anxiety and fear:

- Teachers need to keep an orderly classroom environment as far as possible.

- They need to project calmness themselves, avoiding shouting (which a previously abused child could perceive as threatening).

- They also need to understand what, for this particular child, is likely to provoke anxiety, shame or distress. The trigger might be a particular sanction (or even a reward), changes, surprises, excitement, a school trip, unstructured time, or something that sparks a memory of a traumatic incident. Children who are anxious and find friendships difficult can dread break times. Teachers need to understand the child and make adjustments.

- Most children enjoy the pre-Christmas period at school, when the usual routine is often left behind in favour of special Christmas-related activities and treats. But a child who struggles with change can find this slightly chaotic period in school very stressful, so teachers need to be mindful of this.

- If a child is hypervigilant and cannot concentrate because of anxiety, it may help if the teacher allows her to choose where to sit in the classroom. For example, the child may feel safer if she is sitting close to the teacher or may prefer to sit with her back to the wall where she can see the classroom door, so that she is not stressed by the thought of people coming up behind her.

- Perhaps the most important thing that helps the child feel safe in the classroom is knowing that the teacher "gets" her and understands her difficulties. There are ways that parents can work with the teacher to help with this (see this chapter, and Chapter 5).

Helping a child who is becoming dysregulated

In addition to the points above, some other things that can help a dysregulated child in school are listed below. Each child is different, so it's a question of knowing what works for an individual child:

- a "safe corner" in the classroom or school to retreat to (described below);
- physical effort, e.g. digging, scrubbing;
- activity such as jumping on a trampoline;
- playing with play dough, fidget spinners, etc;
- putting a blanket over the child (there are specially weighted blankets available for this purpose);
- bubble machines;
- rocking chairs;
- music;
- stress balls;
- drumming sessions;
- "brain breaks" – for free time, to play a game or move around – to allow the brain time to process information;
- time outside, e.g. walking or running round the school field or playground.

A "safe corner"

An important way of helping a child to calm down is to provide a physical safe place with a sense of safety, calmness and containment – this can be a sensory room, a pop-up tent or a special corner set up with cushions, blankets and other things that can have a calming effect on children, such as those above.

Ideally, a child should have a way of letting the teacher know when she needs to go to a special place where she feels safe, when the classroom or playground environment feels too overwhelming or threatening. Not all children will recognise when they need to do this, so the teacher/PSA needs to be sufficiently tuned into the child's emotional state to recognise when she needs to be taken there. Older children and young people may be able to recognise for themselves when they need to retreat for a while and should have permission to leave the classroom if necessary to calm down. Some schools have been willing to set up a system for a particular child to notify the teacher that she needs to go there, such as showing a special card.

Recognising behaviour as "communication"

> *He carries the trauma with him very profoundly every second of the day and that's what we struggle to make people understand.*
>
> (Adoptive parent, personal communication)

Biting, hitting, kicking, shouting, swearing, running out of the classroom... For a teacher attempting to teach a class of 30 children, a child who disrupts lessons in this way can make teaching pretty much impossible.

A different approach is needed, which starts with understanding why the child is behaving as she does.

Schools and teachers need to know how to create environments that reduce such behaviour – for the sake of the child, for the sake of the rest of the class, and for their own sake, because the child is clearly under extreme stress and it can also cause great stress for the teacher and other children if they have to deal with it every school day.

Nicola Marshall is an adoptive mother of three teenagers and founder of BraveHeart Education. She explains the need for flexibility:

> *Probably the hardest and most important area for schools to address is our obsession with modifying behaviour. What we have at the moment are systems that essentially work on the premise that children and young people have the same level of respect for authority that they used to have and, indeed, that they all have the same understanding as each other and the ability to change their behaviour when we tell them to.*
>
> *Zone boards, sticker charts, marble jars, sun and dark clouds, house points, incentive schemes, yellow and red cards, isolations, detentions, time outs and exclusions all rely on a child's ability to join the dots between their*

behaviour and the consequences. If I know that when I speed in my car I might kill someone and end up in prison, does it stop me speeding? It should, and most of the time it does, but there are odd occasions when I forget, or maybe my anxiety over being late, or whatever it might be, takes over and drives my behaviour to ignore the rules.

Children and young people who've not had the chance to develop cause and effect thinking and may be operating in the survival part of their brain cannot manage their behaviour just because we move them down the zone board or show them a red card. In fact, for some children, being "on a red" gets them the most attention and that's what they most crave. They need someone to notice that they are struggling and to keep them safe.

Moving away from these punitive, shame-riddled systems will take time and can be messy. We have to concentrate on relationships and understanding the child's experience of school. We may even have to change our approach to certain children, when we consider what their early experiences might have been like.

(Marshall, 2018)

Creating a positive school ethos and culture that is able to promote positive relationships and behaviour for all children, including those with emotional, social and behavioural difficulties, requires teachers and other school staff to understand something about the impact of trauma on the brain, to see behaviour as "communication" and to develop strategies for successful interventions that are based on the importance of attachment, warm and empathic relationships and increasing the child's feelings of safety and decreasing their feelings of anxiety.

Children who may have been deprived of affection and/or harshly punished in early life for getting things wrong are liable to experience an overwhelming sense of humiliation and shame when they are told off (even mildly) or singled out from the rest of the class.

Some schools arrange training for all school staff – teachers, PSAs, supervisors, catering, administration and janitorial staff and after-school providers – so that increasingly all the adults in the school begin to move the conversation from 'what is wrong with this child' to 'what has happened to this child', and look at "challenging" behaviour in a different way. Rather than seeing it as naughtiness, silliness or the child trying to wind them up, they begin to see it as behaviour that the child cannot help, as a sign that the child is dysregulated, or as a throwback to their days of surviving in a dysfunctional family. When this type of training is successful, people are more willing to be flexible and to adopt alternative approaches.

Teachers need to get to know the child in order to get beneath the behaviour and reflect on what is actually going on for him or her, what the message is and what hidden emotions are behind the behaviour. Obviously parents are the ones best placed to help teachers to "get" their son or daughter, so by working with the school you can help bring about change. Teachers then have the opportunity to use more appropriate responses.

Emotional awareness

Children's early adverse experiences can affect their ability to identify, understand and manage their own emotions and to empathise with other people's feelings.

Schools are adopting a wide range of initiatives and interventions that aim to build children's emotional literacy. For example, one approach is called "emotion coaching":

Emotion coaching was first introduced by John Gottman and his colleagues in the USA. Emotion coaching is about helping children to become more aware of their emotions and to manage their own feelings, particularly during instances of misbehaviour. It entails validating children's emotions, setting limits where appropriate and problem-solving with the child to develop more effective behavioural strategies.

In effect, emotion coaching techniques instil the tools that will aid children's ability to self-regulate their emotions and behaviour. It enables practitioners to create an ethos of positive learning behaviour and to have the confidence to de-escalate situations when behaviour is challenging. Emotion coaching provides a value-added dimension to behaviour management strategies and creates opportunities for longer-term solutions to children's well-being and resilience.

(www.bathspa.ac.uk/schools/education/research/emotion-coaching)

Emotion coaching has the potential to help many children, but those more seriously affected by trauma will need more targeted support such as therapy.

Sensory issues

Schools and teachers need to be ready to make adjustments for children with sensory issues.

- As explained earlier, the school or class teacher can set up a "calm area" or cosy nurture room to which the child can withdraw when feeling overwhelmed. Some schools already have such special spaces for students with autism.

- Children who are bothered by noise may find it helpful to wear noise-blocking headphones.

- Some children may need to sit somewhere away from the lights or windows if they find it too bright.

- Those who find the feel of certain items of the school uniform unpleasant might need permission to wear something different.

- Other adjustments might include the child being able to do tasks that help her to avoid the playground at break time, if that is overwhelming for her, or allowing her to eat her lunch somewhere other than the school dining hall.

Every child is unique, and each child will need different adjustments in order to feel comfortable in school or to work well in the classroom. Below is one adoptive mother's account of some of the measures that made a difference for her son, whom she refers to as 'Little Bear'.

'I feel hopeful now'

A couple of weeks ago I blogged about how Little Bear was doing at school, the apparent desire to keep us at arm's length and my concerns about the school's ability to support and educate him. Little Bear's behaviour was spiralling and his teacher was tearing her hair out. It was going badly and I was very worried. Since then I have had several conversations with his teacher, and at parents' evening, and we finally had the big meeting we had been asking for.

The landscape now is very different. I think they are getting more right than they are getting wrong and Little Bear is starting to thrive. I thought it might be helpful to share some of the things we/they have done that have made the difference.

A timetable

Don't ask me why, but when Little Bear started Year 1 (P1) there was no set timetable of what he would be doing each day; sometimes it could be maths then literacy, at other times phonics then maths, etc. His teacher realised after a few weeks that he might cope better if the expectations were clearer and his day was more predictable. They created a timetable for him but things were still going awry. I wondered aloud one day whether Little Bear was able to see the timetable himself. It turned out they were showing him the black and white typed adult version which was, of course, entirely meaningless to him.

Little Bear now has a timetable made up of digital photos of him doing all the different tasks. This is working fabulously.

He knows the routine and seems much happier to get on with what he is meant to be doing. Plus he actually likes the timetable because he is in it and is therefore much more motivated to engage with it.

"Choose" time

As Little Bear finds it difficult to concentrate for any length of time, we agreed that he would do alternate short work tasks with "fun tasks" to keep him on track. The fun task would be used as a carrot in a "now work, then fun task" kind of way. The fun task might also involve moving about to give him a physical/sensory break from sitting still. The fun tasks have been chosen carefully so they are still educational (they might involve developing his play skills or turn-taking or creativity, etc) and are actually motivating to Little Bear, not just perceived to be motivating by an adult.

The choices are presented to Little Bear in photo form (with him in the pictures) and he picks in advance of each work activity.

This is also working brilliantly to the point where some mornings he is now able to complete all the work tasks on his timetable and doesn't need any fun tasks at all.

A consistent approach

None of the above would be working if it wasn't for this. The teacher and teaching assistant (TA/PSA) have now figured out their strategy and are being much clearer with Little Bear. There is no shouting one minute then letting him off with something the next any more. I think they have settled on a calm, firm approach much like we use at home.

They have also realised that Little Bear benefits from some extra rules where other children wouldn't. For example, if he is tired one day and therefore allowed to read just one page instead of three, he will expect that he can do the same thing the next day. If he can find a chink in the armour he will exploit it. However, if there is a blanket rule such as "every day we read three pages", Little Bear knows where he is at and is much happier to adhere to it.

I think his TA was feeling mean about doing this but has found out the hard way that Little Bear actually feels a lot safer when he knows exactly what is expected and adults around him are consistent with their boundaries. If not, his anxiety will spike and his behaviour will become increasingly challenging. Now that he feels safer, he is much more open to learning.

A discipline re-think

The school as a whole were using the "Good To Be Green" behaviour system, which involves children getting an amber warning card when they do something they shouldn't and then a red card if they do something else, or do something violent. Thankfully they did see early on that this didn't work for Little Bear. There are the immediate issues with public shaming but for him the main problem was that once you get an amber or red card you can't work your way back to green that day. Once you've got in some bother and already had a red card, what is the point of trying to control yourself for the rest of the day? You might as well just go for it and do whatever you like. It is a very negative system. Also, Little Bear was getting upset by the card changes because he isn't naughty, he just finds controlling himself really difficult. He was frequently very annoyed with himself for seemingly having failed, which impacted his mood for the rest of the day.

Thankfully school recognised that they couldn't continue with that system for him so came up with a new system, "Magic 1,2,3", to use instead. They didn't want to single Little Bear out from his peers so have changed the system for the whole of his class – a very sensitive gesture, I felt.

I'm not sure that I love "Magic 1,2,3" per se but it has an accidental benefit which is crucial for Little Bear. Basically, the teacher counts each time you do something you shouldn't, so you get three chances to make amends or make a different choice. If after three chances you still haven't co-operated or you have had three separate misdemeanours, you have to sit on the "thinking chair".

Now, I know a lot of parents won't like it because it is basically sitting in the corner. However, for Little Bear it gives him the calm-down time he desperately needs.

I have struggled to get school to understand that when Little Bear is thoroughly pissed off, the last thing he needs is someone lecturing him, talking at him. He needs to sit somewhere quietly until he is ready to talk. At home, we just ask him to sit wherever he is. He sits on the floor and we stay nearby and usually he'll say, 'I'm ready, Mummy,' after about three seconds (a "time-in"). However, it turns out that school weren't ever allowing him this time, so it wasn't any wonder he was nearly blowing a gasket sometimes and going straight from one incident to another.

Sitting on the "thinking chair" gives him just the de-compression he needs. Also, it is in the classroom so he is not isolated or left alone.

I don't think this would be the right thing for every child, but it is suiting Little Bear much better and his behaviour has calmed enormously.

Praise and positive reinforcement

Little Bear's behaviour was becoming such an issue in school that I felt all the positives were getting lost. They had pretty much got to the point of thinking there weren't any. Apart from me pointing this out, I don't really know what changed, but the teacher and TA have certainly got better at looking for the positives and making a big fuss about them.

Again, this wouldn't work for children who can't handle praise but Little Bear really thrives off it. School has cottoned on to this and whenever Little Bear tries hard or produces something good, they encourage him to share it with the class. He absolutely loves this and I think it helps his peers to see him as someone who is successful, not just someone they think is naughty.

Working as a team

I do feel that school have recognised that they had cut us out of the loop and are now keen to include us more. I think they can see the benefits and that when there are meetings, it is not because we want to tell them off or be difficult, it is because we genuinely want to work in partnership. We have two further meetings arranged, which has allayed a lot of my concerns.

We have agreed common goals, such as to extend Little Bear's reading from three pages to four in one sitting and to encourage him to work independently for two minutes instead of one. The goals are achievable and measurable, which is exactly as they should be and because we are working on them at home and at school I'm sure they will be met more quickly.

A key part of the meeting we had was to share information about Little Bear's history with his new TA. She didn't know how long he had been with us, what his developmental starting point was, etc. It would have been much more helpful for her to know all this at the start because then she could have adjusted her expectations accordingly from the outset. However, we can't undo the past and at least she is now armed with all the facts.

Communication

To help school to communicate with us in a way that works for us, they invited us to have a discussion and be clear about what we actually want to know. We have agreed that they will comment on Little Bear's behaviour each day and how he has got on with his independent working, hopefully in a 'one thing that went well and perhaps a thing that didn't go so well' sort of way.

Lateral thinking

School have been great about being open to different ideas and ways of doing things. Sometimes they still struggle to get Little Bear to have a go at things; he might flatly refuse or say he hates whatever it is. They have agreed to try things like offering Little Bear the opportunity to go and show his brother his work if he tries hard at it. I think he will be extremely motivated to do that and Big Bear is happy to be involved and relishes the added responsibility.

As the TA directly asked us for some advice on how to manage this, we were also able to talk about wondering and empathising, for example: 'It must be hard to get your work done if you hate English. I wonder if that's because you find it tricky' rather than a dismissive, 'You don't hate it.'

It meant more to us than they probably realised to be asked and to be considered a source of knowledge about our child. The head teacher also apologised to us and admitted they had got the transition badly wrong. He asked what could be done differently next time.

We left the meeting feeling reassured, listened to and that Little Bear is in safe hands. They might not get it right all the time but at least they know that and are not afraid to admit it and ask for help.

I feel hopeful now.

(Blogfox14, 2017)

Encouraging friendships

More and more schools are addressing children's social difficulties and recognising the need to promote kind and caring behaviour, to encourage children's friendships and tackle bullying.

Some of their approaches include:

- nurture groups;
- a buddy system, where the teacher puts in place special friends or friendship groups for children who are new to the school or who are struggling to make friends;
- peer mentors – often children from higher years in the school who can work with younger ones to encourage friendships or to give them someone to talk to if they are worried or upset;
- playground games organised by trained lunchtime supervisors to help children make friends, to provide structure at breaktime and to reduce conflict in the playground;
- lunchtime and after-school clubs for Lego, ICT (information and communications technology), computer games, etc, so that vulnerable students have genuine options for somewhere to go if they don't like the playground or the football field, or if they find it easier to interact with other children over a structured activity.

When your child has formed some friendships, it is important to "cultivate" them by ensuring they have the opportunity for playdates, tea after school, etc.

(Karen Wilkins, adoptive mother)

I think that things in friendships are complicated and figuring it out is hard. I've found sometimes talking about relationships and friendships difficult. I think this is because it reminds me of when I was little I had a different family and friends. I think people who haven't been adopted don't have the same feelings because they have not experienced the same things in their past. My friends who are not adopted talk about their past quite a lot, for adopted people this can be harder.

(Anna, age 11, adopted at 3½)

Recognising trauma triggers and sensitive issues in the curriculum

Common curriculum areas that adoptive parents often mention as tricky for their children are: being asked to bring in pictures of the child as a baby (which you may not have); writing about your early life; assemblies about maltreated children (e.g. by the NSPCC); and being asked to draw a family tree.

In secondary school, for example, discussion around genetics, such as 'What colour eyes do your parents have and what colour are yours?' can enhance an adopted child's feeling of being different from peers who are not adopted. Lessons about drugs and alcohol can stir up unhappy memories of birth relatives misusing these and also make a child worry about developing the same problems. Sex education lessons could be uncomfortable or upsetting for a child who was sexually abused in early life, as could lessons about the effect of alcohol in pregnancy, for young people with FASD. The quotes from children, below, illustrate this.

> *I've had the NSPCC come to school…and they were talking all about kids being abused and neglected and I was quite young but it hit me really hard – like – wait, I've actually been abused and neglected…I went home crying and crying to my mum because I could not understand what had happened. But if my mum had been told beforehand the NSPCC were coming into school*

and they're going to talk about this, she would have been able to tell me the information I needed to know instead of me finding out, then going home crying and not understanding anything.

(Adopted young person speaking in a film produced by Coram Life Education)

Some of the things we have covered in class/our work have been difficult for me. An example is Macbeth because this has lots of reference to knives, and that is something I don't like thinking about because it reminds me of something in the past. Sometimes the subjects we cover in class, like drugs and alcohol, can result in my friends asking me questions, they are hard to answer because it sounds all weird to them because it's not their experience of life.

I think teachers could make these things better by learning more about it themselves so they can explain it to other people better. Like drugs and alcohol, the teacher needs to understand more about it and how it affects people – not just saying 'don't do it'; because in my adopted family we have experience of our birth mothers drinking alcohol and we know how that has affected the children they gave birth to. I understand it's not just about the person that drinks or takes drugs but can also be about the child and others around them. My teachers don't seem to understand this, or even seem to want to know, or are interested to know, because they don't understand or want to know about peoples' lives. I don't think they understand how it makes me feel. With friendships, maybe they could find a way to talk to people who are finding it difficult to help them, and find a way to talk to the class about it to help people understand.

(Anna, age 11, adopted at 3½)

If teachers know about these triggers they can try to help your child avoid them in the classroom. So, as a parent you will need to make the school aware (although not necessarily give all the details) so that they can make some adjustments (see Chapter 5). If events do occur, they need to be treated sensitively and used as learning experiences for everyone involved. Some subjects have to be covered in the curriculum, so a discussion between the school and parents might be needed about how to approach these subjects so as to have minimum impact on the adopted child.

Schools need to be aware of how the curriculum can trigger questions for adopted children. Our school consults adopters and foster carers before they show any of the sex education-type videos. Incidentally, I do believe there is an opportunity to provide schools with an adoption-friendly version of this! The video our school uses is very dated and does not reflect the diversity of families in modern Britain. Quotes such as, 'We all come from our mummy's tummy' can be very confusing for an adopted child who knows they didn't come from their mum's tummy.

(Karen Wilkins, adoptive mother)

As explained in Chapter 2, children who have missed out on early nurturing experiences may be delayed in their emotional development and have the needs and behaviour of a much younger child. So it is helpful for the teacher to adjust expectations and use approaches targeted to the child's emotional age rather than her actual chronological age.

Helping a child with executive functioning difficulties

For a child who struggles to organise herself, remember things, follow instructions and manage tasks, these approaches can help:

- Having a mentor/one-to-one time with a member of the school staff at the start and end of the school day or with whom she can "check in" at certain points to make sure she has all she needs, has understood homework tasks, knows where to go next, and so on.

- When giving instructions to the child, the teacher can use the child's name first, to get her attention; then give precise, rather than general instructions, such as 'Emily, go to the changing room and put on your gym kit and trainers' rather than just 'Get ready for gym.'

- Tasks should be broken down into manageable chunks to help the child understand how to tackle them.

- The school can keep spare gym kits, pencil cases and so on for children who have forgotten to bring their own.

- Visual timetables at home and school, which show the child in pictures and with simple words what she needs to do and at what time (e.g. getting ready for school) or what exactly will be the sequence of events on that day in school. (The pictures on the visual timetable can even be photographs of the child doing the various activities, which will help give her ownership and help her relate to it.)

- Together with your child, you can help by getting her school clothes and school bag ready every evening so that they are there for her in the morning, with no last-minute panics. Get her into a routine of packing her bag and checking off a list of all the things she needs to take each day (consulting the visual timetable).

- Help your child with time management of homework, prioritising urgent tasks but ensuring that she doesn't forget the less urgent tasks.

Celebrating success

Some children are very fearful of making mistakes because they have learned in their early life that doing something wrong will incur an adult's anger or punishment. Fear of making mistakes can lead to children being unable to take part in classroom activities; they are too anxious that they will fail.

Finding something they are good at can really help. If they do not excel in the classroom, they may enjoy music or school sport, or joining a choir or out-of-school activity or club such as swimming, Brownies or Scouts, or keeping a pet. Anything out of school that helps build their self-esteem will have a knock-on effect in school too.

The teacher can give your child tasks that she can do in the classroom to build a sense of achievement:

- Set the child up to succeed. Give her tasks that you know she can do, so she can build on these small successes.
- Reassure the child that making mistakes is just part of learning.
- Praise her for trying.
- Ask her to help the teacher.
- Ask her to help a younger child.

Some children find praise hard to take, so it needs to be chosen and delivered with care. If a child cannot accept praise or sabotages attempts to reward her, you (and the teacher) need to find other ways to do it – for example, praise what she has done rather than praising the child herself: 'That little boy was so pleased when you shared the Lego with him' rather than 'You are a good girl.' Praising in private might be easier for the child rather than in front of everyone, and praising in non-verbal ways with a high-five or pat on the back can work well. Being specific is also good: 'I like the way you have used those bright colours in your picture' rather than simply: 'That's lovely.'

Attachment Ambassadors

Some schools are seeing the advantage of having someone who can be the key link between school and home for children who find school difficult. They get to know the parents/carers and their child, and act as a mediator between them and school. This may be part of the role of an Attachment Ambassador or any staff member responsible for promoting the resilience of vulnerable children and building a nurturing ethos in the school. Many schools are now realising the benefit of including adopted children in the support arrangements they have in place for other vulnerable children.

Case study: one school's journey to becoming attachment-friendly

Jennifer Nock is a chartered psychologist and educator who has worked for over 30 years in a wide range of education and additional support for learning settings, with educators, children and young people, families and fostering and adoption agencies.

Writing in *SEN Magazine*, she described how one school put into practice its resolve to provide effective, lasting support to pupils with attachment issues. This was Hope School in Liverpool, a school for boys aged 5–14 with social, emotional and mental health difficulties. The head teacher wanted to explore a more nurturing approach to behaviour than the traditional reward and sanctions-type methods that the school was using at that time.

Over the following several months, the senior leadership team (SL Team) developed a strategic plan to improve attachment-friendly practice. Initial training on attachment and trauma was delivered to the whole staff, including the leadership team. The SL Team looked at what staff were doing currently and how they might change their behaviour management methods:

The SL Team prioritised developing adult calmness, self-control and modelling appropriate behaviour. They also advised that staff avoid getting into tit-for-tat exchanges with pupils, and reduce any interactions that raised children's stress levels, as these often back pupils into a corner from which they cannot escape. Instead, staff were asked to offer two good choices, for example: 'Would you like me to sit with you, or are you better on your own?' Staff were asked to give instructions in a calm and positive manner, where phrases like, 'Don't get the Lego on the floor' become 'Keep the Lego on the table, please'; 'Don't get stressed!' becomes 'Deep breaths and slow breathing'. Staff were also asked to increase the use of proximity [e.g. having the pupil sit near them]*, the pupil's name and frequent firm, respectful touch, as these often have a calming and grounding effect on dysregulated pupils. Four pupils were identified to receive an intensive intervention, including the allocation of key workers to support each of the pupils.*

For each boy, a targeted programme of intervention included a daily meet-and-greet session on entry to school, a daily relationship-based play session with the key worker and a sensory and body work programme. Individual interventions included a weekly sand tray session, use of calm box activities when early signs of over-arousal were observed, daily massage and emotional literacy games and activities.

(Nock, undated)

Key points

- There's a growing awareness of why some adopted children struggle with school. Understanding where a child's difficulties come from is the first step towards being able to offer the right kind of support.

- Professionals in the fields of trauma, attachment and FASD, academics, adoption support organisations and adoptive parents are working hard to get the message through to schools and teachers across the country so that they can make the adjustments children need and support them to achieve all they are capable of.

- Nurturing Approaches, ACE-Aware, Attachment-Aware and Trauma Informed Practice are all approaches used in schools that indicate that there is knowledge and understanding of challenges faced by adopted children.

- The more that you, as an adoptive parent, know and understand about your child's needs and behaviour, and the techniques that work for her, the more you will be able to help guide the school.

4 Choosing and starting a new primary school

When is the best time to start school?

The school year begins in mid-August (the exact date varies between local authorities), and children normally start in Primary 1 (P1) between the ages of four-and-a-half and five-and-a-half. This means that if your child has a birthday between March and the start of the autumn term in August, they will have reached the age of five before they start school. If their birthday falls after the start of the autumn term in August, or between September and February, they will be expected to start P1 at the age of four.

Delaying when your child starts primary school

If your child is still four years old on the date they are due to start primary school, you can defer your child's entry to primary school by a year.

If your child was born in January or February, and you do not believe they are ready to start school when they are four-and-a-half, the process is relatively straightforward. You make your local authority and/or catchment school aware of your decision to defer entry, and your request will be automatically approved. Your child will then start school the following year at the age of five-and-a-half. In addition, if you decide to defer entry for a child with a January or February birthday, they will be automatically entitled to an additional year of funded pre-school education.

However, the situation is slightly more complex if your child was born between mid-August and December. You can still request to defer their entry to primary school until the following year, via your local authority and/or catchment school, but it is at the discretion of the local authority and there may be a process to go through. You may be asked for your reasons for wishing to defer entry and asked to support your reasons with evidence. If you choose to defer entry in these circumstances, your child will not be automatically entitled to another year of funded pre-school education. You will have to apply to your local authority for an additional year – it's at their discretion.

> *Allan's birthday is in November and he was very behind emotionally, cognitively, socially and in some motor skills, so I felt he was not ready to start school when he was aged four. I applied to my local authority to defer until next year and they turned me down, even though I had a letter of support from my adoption agency. Allan was at a private nursery which, I discovered, had little experience in supporting applications. Luckily, I was switching Allan to a school nursery and they quickly acknowledged that deferral would be the right thing for him. They worked with me to put together a plan to support Allan's development in nursery, getting ready for starting school a year later. My reapplication was successful.*
>
> (Meg, adoptive mother and single parent)

Many adoptive parents also feel that their children need extra time at home to catch up on developmental stages they may have missed and to strengthen their attachment to their parents. Thus, they take advantage of deferral if their child's birthday allows. If your child's birthday falls outside the deferral criteria, it is difficult to postpone starting school unless you home educate (see Chapter 6). You would need to provide evidence relating to all aspects of your child's development, and professionals involved would have to agree with you that deferred entry is an appropriate intervention for the identified issues and in your child's best interests. It may be more beneficial to ask for an assessment of your child's needs (if this has not been carried out already) and start school at the usual time with an appropriate support package in place. If your child has started school before they are placed with you, this decision has already been made. However, you would face similar difficulties if you feel your child would benefit from repeating a year or delaying moving to high school.

The main reasons why local authorities have a general rule that children should be educated with their chronological age group include:

- As they mature, a child may realise that the rest of their class are of a different age, causing a feeling of difference and stigma.

- The child may begin puberty at a different time from their classmates, which could be confusing for them.

- Your child will be eligible to leave school at 16 and may not have completed their education or had the opportunity to gain any qualifications.

- The needs of a child with significant additional support needs are unlikely to change substantially in 12 months.
- Children learn a great deal from their peers, and receive social, emotional, and academic support from each other.
- Evidence suggests that placing children/students in a different year group rarely makes a positive difference and can lead to negative long-term effects (Highland Council, 2019). (This was not research on adopted children.)

Louise was placed with us aged three. Her birthday is in February, but we thought that deferring her entry to P1 would be beneficial in helping her attach to us and for her development. She was quite delayed and couldn't talk when she came to us. Our social worker advised that time spent with us in the early years was "money in the bank" for later years. We had no difficulty in getting the agreement of our local authority. We think that being one of the oldest in her year has been helpful for her confidence. There was an issue recently with her having to go into a composite P6/7 class as one of the oldest in the P6 year. Composites in our local authority are based on age. So, this has been quite an advanced class and she has felt out of her depth.

(Claire, adoptive mother)

Jamie was placed with us at 16 weeks and adopted at four-and-a-half. He had been exposed to alcohol in the womb and also suffered neglect and physical abuse. We were aware that school was going to be a challenge for him and made a careful choice of primary school after a lot of research. Unfortunately, there was very little understanding of his difficulties and many opportunities to recognise and build on his strengths were missed. We had also been on the CAMHS waiting list for three years. By the end of P4, he was behind academically and presenting as immature compared to his peers. We really felt he would benefit from repeating P4, but our local authority was not supportive. We were aware of the issues associated with being educated out with his peer group but we still felt that repeating a year would allow Jamie to mature. We contacted a neighbouring authority which had a care experienced team in place and a head of nurture, and they agreed to him repeating P4 in one of their schools. They had an understanding of where he was coming from.

(Grace, adoptive mother)

Starting school in a pre-adoptive placement

The next section, 'Choosing a primary school', provides advice on how to decide whether a particular school is likely to meet the needs of your child. If your child is in a pre-adoptive placement with you when he reaches school age and you do not consider your catchment school to be suitable for him, you will need to consult with the local authority responsible for your child and should seek advice and support from your adoption agency or other advice body. If your child has already started school before he moves into a pre-adoptive placement with you, he may remain at his existing school or, if this is not practical, move to your catchment school. Again, if you do not consider your catchment school to be suitable for your child, there will need to be agreement in the team around the child on which school will be most suitable. Hopefully you will have had an interval between approval and matching to do some preliminary research.

The information below is adapted from an information sheet originally produced by the Cambridgeshire Virtual School.

If your child has to change school, this is an additional, major transition for him, and it is important that all parties prepare for him starting a new school and help to ease the transition. The primary concern in a pre-adoptive placement is for the child to develop relationships with their new family. He needs to feel safe and secure. This is likely to mean a short period when he is not in education. The aim should be to minimise the impact that this may have on his progress and attainment, as well as to ensure a smooth transition into the new school. The appropriateness of all the strategies below should be considered in light of each child, family and school's unique situation. This is a difficult situation for prospective adoptive parents, because they do not yet have parental rights and responsibilities for their child. These will lie with the placing authority or possibly even the birth parents.

Before the child moves in with the pre-adoptive family

- The choice of destination school should be discussed with the social workers for the child and prospective adopters and possibly others involved with the child, for example, foster carers. In addition, if the parents' local authority has a virtual school head, they could also be consulted.

- The prospective adopters should scrutinise the websites of their catchment school and any other possible schools and should organise a visit to look around. The schools should provide the prospective adopters with a prospectus and any other relevant documentation. This is an opportunity to find out about the school's experience of supporting children who have experienced early trauma or who have attachment needs.

- Once a collective decision has been made about the most appropriate school, it also needs to be decided whether the child's social worker or the prospective adopters will complete and submit the admission form.

- It may be appropriate for the family to visit the existing school to meet with the teacher to get a flavour of the child's learning profile. However, it is likely that the child will be unaware of the match at this point. Therefore this may need to be after school hours, or alternatively, at a time during the day when the child is not on the school site, so that the child does not inadvertently come into contact with the prospective adopters. The teacher or head teacher should have been attending looked after child (LAC) reviews and other meetings about the child (or at least sending a report), so there should be a timeline of information available about the child's education history. Some local authorities are starting to use child appreciation events post matching, where prospective adopters meet with adults who have been involved in the child's life. In addition to the current foster carers, these might include previous foster carers, nursery workers and teachers.

- A transition meeting should be held that includes the current and new school, current carers and prospective adopters. This should focus on the current school's and carers' experience of what works well, both in terms of supporting the child's emotional needs and educational progress. It should detail transition arrangements, with rough timescales for visits and starting school. It will be possible to alter these at any stage, but having them in place early can minimise drift.

  It is important that everyone has a common understanding of names used by the child, when talking to and about their adoptive and birth families. Consideration should be given to the surname by which the child will be known (this could be either the birth or adoptive family name – the social workers will need to advise on any legal issues).

- The current school should consider appropriate leaving arrangements, e.g. peers to make cards, possibly purchasing a book that the class has focused on as a gift, leavers' assembly. The child's "key adult" will be especially important, leading up to the change of placement and school. The school needs to be receptive to the fact that the child may need additional reassurance and "nurture time", while also recognising the need for consistency and routine. It may be a good idea to have an age-appropriate, direct conversation with the child along the lines of: 'You may have a wobble, this will be hard but everyone is going to help you settle and do your best.'

- The current school should ensure that they collect photos, work, videos, etc of the child's time at school, which can form part of their life story work.

Once the child has moved in with the pre-adoptive family but before starting at the new school

- The pre-adoptive family could look at the new school website with the child and consider any questions that the child may have about the school.

- The pre-adoptive family could organise a visit with the child to look around the school and ask any questions that they may have. The transition meeting should have given the new school an opportunity to find out about the child's interests, e.g. if he is keen on sport, the tour of the school could incorporate a focus on the sporting resources and provision on offer within the school.

- It may be appropriate for the school to prepare a book for the child, with photos of key adults and areas of the school, to share at home. It may be possible to organise for the child to take home a class teddy, which they could bring back to school when they start. For an older child, it may be helpful for the class teacher to create an "all about me" sheet for the child to have. This can help the child to quickly feel more comfortable with the teacher.

- The school can provide the family with information on the themes/topics that are being covered and ideas of how the family could support pre-learning, ready for when the child starts school. This may include experiences and active learning, e.g. if the theme is autumn:

  - go to the local park;
  - play in the leaves;
  - collect leaves for a collage;
  - take photos of autumnal things, e.g. conkers, bare trees, etc;

- create prints or leaf rubbings;
- sort leaves by colour, size, shape;
- visit the library and get non-fiction books on autumn and related story books to share at home;
- carry out internet research on the seasons.

The purpose of immersing the child in these sorts of activities is to enable bonding with the family and familiarity with the local environment, as well as exposure to vocabulary and experiences that should help the child feel that they have valuable contributions to make when they start school. It may be appropriate for the child to bring into school some of the things that they have completed at home to share with their teacher/key person when they start school. It is important that there is no stress or pressure associated with the activities; you will need to judge how much and which activities are most appropriate to your child and family.

To be in place for when the child starts the new school

- Actions discussed at the transition meeting should be in place.
- The new school should consider organising a "buddy" to be with the child in the first few days.
- The child should have a key adult/s who will "touch base" with them regularly.
- Schools should bear in mind that "suddenly becoming parents" could mean that parents may have missed out on the events and experiences that many birth parents will have had, such as developing friendships with other parents in the community through antenatal classes, attending play groups or new parents' meetings at school, where they have been exposed to approaches to early learning. It may be appropriate for the class teacher or relevant member of staff to meet with the parents to explain how the school approaches reading, phonics, writing, maths, etc, and how the parents can best support learning at home. Parents will also need information on general school rules and routines. You may welcome school support in meeting other parents and becoming part of the community.

- Schools should consider how best to develop home/school communication; parents may have lots of questions to begin with and will also need effective communication as to how their child is settling in.

- Schools must monitor the educational progress of a child who is looked after, and this should be discussed at the co-ordination meetings that will be held between social workers and prospective adopters until a looked after child is formally adopted.

(Adapted from information produced by Cambridgeshire Virtual School)

Choosing a primary school

You may be thinking about this at an early stage if you plan to place your child in nursery, as some primary schools have nursery classes attached. The Government guide provides a useful starting point (www.gov.scot/publications/choosing-school-guide-parents-nov-16).

Each local authority is divided into catchment areas for mainstream primary and secondary schools, and each school is either denominational (linked to a particular religion) or non-denominational (not linked to any particular religion). Your home address will have a catchment denominational and non-denominational primary and secondary school. Most Scottish councils publish catchment area maps on their websites. In the first instance, your child should be given a place at your catchment school. You can request a place at another school, but whether this request is granted depends on the availability of free places. There is a right of appeal if your request is not granted. More information on this is provided in Chapter 6 under 'Admissions'.

There is a 'find a school' tool in the Parentzone area of the Education Scotland website. This includes all schools in Scotland: state funded, independent and grant aided, and nursery, primary, secondary, special and Gaelic schools. For each school, it provides contact details, links to school websites where available, and other information (see Useful resources). There is also the School Information Dashboard, part of Smarter Scotland (www.education.gov.scot/parentzone/my-school/school-information-dashboard), which provides very detailed information about all the publicly funded schools. Choosing the right school to meet your child's needs isn't always an easy decision and your catchment school will not necessarily be the best choice. The previous chapters will have helped to give you an idea of the kind of things schools and teachers can do to make school life better for adopted children. School websites can often provide a lot of insight into a school's ethos. The stories they present and what they celebrate can be revealing. It's really helpful to talk to other adopters, especially if they live in your area, to learn from their experiences. If your most recent experience of school is having been a pupil yourself(!), it can be helpful to get involved with a local school in a volunteering capacity to gain some idea of how schools operate these days.

Arrange a meeting with the head teacher of the school you are considering for your child, so you can explain the issues he might have and the kind of behaviours the teachers might see. Be up front about any difficulties so that the school can work out whether it will be able to support him. If it baulks at this first stage, then you will know it is not the right place for your child.

Below are some key questions to ask school staff when you visit a primary school. Many of the points apply to both primary and secondary, but secondary schools will have different approaches (see Chapter 7).

Key questions for primary schools

It is difficult to know what to look for when choosing a school. Not all of these suggested questions will be relevant for every child and you will have specific questions in relation to your child. It's unlikely that any school will be doing all of these; look for flexible schools that are willing to listen and learn and are proactive about developing support to meet each child's needs.

Have staff received training on any of: attachment, nurturing approach, impact of early trauma and loss, ACEs, FASD?

Who was involved in the training? For example:

- Did senior leadership attend?
- Were SLTs and PSAs included?
- Was it cascaded to playground and lunchtime supervisors?
- What has been the impact throughout the school?

How does the school provide consistent key relationships for children with attachment needs?

For example:

- named members of staff as key workers for children, with quality one-to-one time scheduled into the child's day or week, with particular attention to the times when the child is most vulnerable;
- staff who are aware of how to let the child know that they are held in mind;
- ways to help children stay connected, e.g. a postcard in the holidays?

Is there a safe base for children when they need to calm down or regulate?

- Is there a nurture group and how do they prioritise children to be part of this?
- Is it used as a planned daily intervention?
- Is there a nurture space or calming zone that children can access as and when needed with a key member of staff?

What is the school's ethos and culture?

- What language is used in school policies? For example, do they talk about "promoting positive behaviour" rather than "managing challenging behaviour", in line with Government guidance (Scottish Government, 2018).
- Does the school appear to follow a whole-school, restorative and supportive approach rather than a punitive one? For example, do they recognise the punitive nature of classroom strategies such as yellow/red card, sun/cloud and their reliance on children understanding cause and effect?
- Does the school see behaviour as communication, and focus on meeting those needs?
- What is the school's approach to exclusion?

What support is in place for children who find unstructured times difficult?

For example:

- Is there an indoor lunch club for more vulnerable children, where they can develop their social skills, or calm down and relax?
- Do the playground supervisors organise structured games in the playground?
- Are there systems for children who want to play with friends, e.g. a buddy system or a friendship bench?

How does the school provide structure and consistency?

For example:

- sticking to the timetable at Christmas and ends of terms;
- letting parents and children know as soon as possible about staff changes and supply teachers;
- providing a schedule for parents to prepare the child at home;
- using visual timetables to let children know about upcoming changes.

How does the school share the information you give them about your child's background and needs?

For example:

- systems;
- meetings, policies, etc;
- If this is on a "need to know" basis, how is this decided and clarified with everyone, including parents?

How does the school share information with parents?

For example:

- Does the class teacher speak to parents at the end of the day, or call home?
- Are staff able to email parents if needed?
- Is there a text message system, e.g. to notify parents about snow days?
- How does the school connect adoptive parents together?
- How active are the Parent Council and Parent Forum?

- Are meetings of the Parent Council and Parent Forum included in newsletters and on the school website?

How has the school used any additional funding?

- How has the school used its Pupil Equity Funding (PEF)?
- Has the school been involved in any initiatives funded from the Care Experienced Children and Young People's Fund (CECYPF)?
- Is the funding used for social and emotional interventions or only for learning?

How does the school support children who find it difficult to manage their feelings?

For example:

- nurture group;
- calm boxes;
- a calming zone within the school;
- emotion regulation skills teaching and coaching;
- anger management training;
- empathy from all staff;
- social skills groups.

How does the school manage curriculum hotspots, i.e. issues that might trigger your child?

For example:

- baby photos and family trees, looking like parents, eye colour, etc;
- cards for Mother's Day and Father's Day;
- topics that involve death or separation, e.g. children being evacuated in World War II;
- curriculum focus on drugs, alcohol and pregnancy;
- having police officers or NSPCC staff visit the school to talk to children;

- special events/assemblies, such as for Children in Need;
- set reading texts that include scary storylines, trauma, losses, etc.

(Adapted from information produced by PAC-UK (Post Adoption Centre), www.pac-uk.org)

Even if the school is not doing everything it could be, and no school can be perfect, you may be able to work with it to help the staff understand your child. If the school is open to listening, you may be able to collaborate with certain key members of staff to bring about changes in the school's approach that will benefit your child and other children as well. Read below how one adoptive parent encouraged her child's school to become more attachment/trauma/FASD-aware and adoption-friendly:

Our big school adventure

Our adopted daughter Niamh was placed with us aged two-and-a-half. We could see from her Form E that she had siblings with diagnoses of ADHD and there was a family history of drug and alcohol abuse, and nearly every adverse childhood experience (ACE) on the list, but to be honest, there had been nothing in our preparation groups about how these could affect children and families long term, although our social worker did give me a book on drugs and alcohol when I asked for more information. Looking back, I realise that our social worker was very rigorous in our home study about how we handled difficult situations and our family support, and I'm sure she had Niamh in mind, although nothing was said.

And so it begins…

I'm the kind of person who likes to be prepared. Our social worker assumed we would send Niamh to a Catholic school, as me and my husband had both been educated in Catholic schools. However, I investigated other options and decided that our non-denominational catchment school would be best for Niamh. The nursery, primary and after school provision were all on the same campus, it was within walking distance and I had heard good reports about it from other parents. Niamh started nursery at three-and-a-half, and I met with the nursery manager before she went to give them some of her history. Niamh loved nursery, but we did receive regular phone calls about incidents and her behaviour. The staff were excellent though, and they felt she was ready for school and organised a good enhanced transition for her.

Unfortunately, six months into P1, Niamh's mental health was suffering. She was very down, and we started to experience child-to-parent violence. Her most difficult time of day was bedtime. We always followed the same routine, but it made no difference whether or not she had a bath, there appeared to be no rhyme or reason for it, but most nights we would have two hours of full-on physical violence. Everything she could lay her hands upon was used as a weapon. We had to remove everything from her bedroom apart from the bed and bedside cabinet, for everyone's safety. After the two hours of hitting, kicking, spitting, etc, all she wanted to do was be cradled to sleep. Looking back now, I think a lot of this was her anger and frustration at not being able to articulate how she was feeling, and the only way she knew how to communicate at that point was through behaviour and lashing out. We realised that she really wasn't ready for the stricter classroom regime and was struggling to fit in.

I am a qualified counsellor and I thought that counselling might help Niamh, even though she was so young. We accessed therapy through CrossReach, partially funded by our local authority (thanks to advocacy from our brilliant social worker), which included Theraplay, art therapy and role playing. It helped Niamh enormously (and me – I needed counselling too). We could have accessed free counselling through the school but would have had to wait two months. We didn't feel the situation could wait!

Fortunately, at the same time a new Principal Inclusion Teacher started at the school. She was very experienced and "got" Niamh straight away. For the next three years, she was Niamh's "safe adult", where she could go if she felt overwhelmed. This relationship was key to her progressing in school and she began to be able to recognise herself when her anxiety levels were high. This teacher also set up a nurture room and Niamh was one of the first group of six children who were put forward for it. In the nurture or "lighthouse" room, children with different additional support needs were taught in a very different way and with a ratio of six pupils to two teachers. Niamh continued in the Nurture room until the end of P3, and I truly believe that had this facility not been set up, our daughter would have had to be removed and home schooled, as her behaviour when overwhelmed is to lash out, kick and hit.

Managing change

During these years, there had been school reorganisations, so P4 meant a change of campus. We were shown the draft enhanced transition, but had to go back to the school and explain just how difficult this was going to be for Niamh. For example, when we moved her bedroom from the box room to the next door, bigger bedroom, we planned it for six months and she made all the decisions about it. She had outgrown the smaller room and was really up for the move. However, on the day, it took nearly 13 hours to actually accomplish it. Within five minutes of starting, she said that she wanted the big room to be exactly the same as the small room. Thankfully, the wall transfers were transferable! We went at her pace and reproduced a mirror-image room. Even with all this, she slept on the floor for two nights in the bigger room because the bed was in a different position. Fortunately, the school was understanding and revised the transition plan. The nurture room staff took her to the new campus every day until she had thoroughly explored every corner of every room. She has one-to-one support and has thrived in P4, where she has an adapted curriculum of learning for two hours every morning and developing social relationships in the afternoons through different activities including baking, dog walking and animal care. We used the Care Experienced Children and Young People's Fund for a 'Relax – Kids' worker in P3 and for art therapy in P4.

Secrets of our "success"

- *Preparation – you can never be too prepared. Start before nursery if you have that option. Do the research, speak to other parents. Don't assume information will be passed on. I always do a typed-up handover at the start of each term as I have found that information isn't passed from one year to the next and things can change dramatically.*

- *Relationships are key – cultivate relationships with key people like the head teacher (they control the money and the ethos of the school) and the Principal Inclusion Teacher (or similar) as well as the class teacher. The class teacher will probably change every year. More senior staff will hopefully be around for longer.*

- *Connection – make it a priority to keep that school/home connection going (just like you do with your child). Try and respect what the school does and keep an open mind. Find common approaches and language that can be used at home and at school. Keep school up to date with what is happening at home and feed back to them if your child is being returned home in a very dysregulated state. Try and work together to identify what works and what can be done differently.*

The "adventure" continues

Now at the start of P5 (post Covid lockdown), we are still in a state of uncertainty. The funding for Niamh's one-to-one support is not guaranteed, and in spite of strong indications of FASD and a very detailed report from TESSA of what is needed to keep her learning in a mainstream school, we still have to advocate for her and be incredibly persistent. It would be lovely to be able to sit back and leave it to the professionals, but I don't think that will be happening any time soon, and the transition to high school is starting to loom...

(Maria, adoptive mother)

Education outwith mainstream school

Unless there are "exceptional circumstances", the presumption is that local authorities provide education to all children in mainstream schools[1] (see https://www.gov.scot/publications/guidance-presumption-provide-education-mainstream-setting). The exceptional circumstances are where:

- a mainstream school would not suit a child's ability or aptitude;
- providing education in a mainstream school would negatively affect the learning of other children in the school;
- placing the child in a mainstream school would cost an unreasonable amount.

So inclusion is to be the norm, but in the context of GIRFEC it is also necessary to look at the needs of each individual child to see if their mainstream school is meeting or can meet them. Mainstream school is not the best option for every child. The question of whether a child needs to move outwith mainstream education can be a difficult and emotionally charged decision for parents. (See Enquire's Factsheet, *School Placements*: www.enquire.org.uk/publications/school-placements.)

---

1 The Standards in Scotland's Schools etc. Act 2000

Sometimes it is clear-cut, but in other cases it may gradually become evident that mainstream school is not the right place, even with all the extra support the school can provide. If this is the case, there are three main options:

Special school

Special schools often contain specialist support services and facilities, and teachers may have a specialist qualification or experience in teaching children with particularly complex needs. There are local authority run schools and a number of independent or grant-aided special schools. The most suitable school for your child may not necessarily be in your local area and sometimes a dual or split placement may be suggested between the local mainstream and a special school.

Special unit or learning base attached to a mainstream school

These offer some of the services of special schools, but in a mainstream setting. Children may be taught full-time or part-time in the unit, or the unit may provide staff to support the child in the classroom.

Residential school

If your child's needs are very complex, then you may need to consider this option. Residential schools offer a range of services that provide for all of a child's needs. Reasons for considering residential school might include geographical access to a very specialised provision, or the effect on the rest of the family of meeting your child's complex needs.

My son had quite a turbulent time in mainstream primary school. He has FASD and did not receive the high level of support he needed; his school experience was made worse by unaddressed bullying, huge gaps in learning and low self-esteem. He was lost in an education system that did not fully understand and was totally inappropriate for him.

I was in the process of making a placing request for a residential school placement, even though I had been advised it was unlikely to be granted, when my son's behaviour spiralled out of control. He was 11 and we could no longer keep him safe. He was posing a risk not only to himself, but to others as well. It was so difficult, but I had to beg social services to take on responsibility for him and fund a therapeutic residential school placement.

> *They agreed due to the escalating level of risk he posed. This meant I had to sign a voluntary care order and I felt broken, that I had given up on my son and that I was losing him.*
>
> *But it was the right decision for me, him and our wider family. Fifteen months later, he is a different child – happy, achieving, reflective and having the time of his life. When he started his new school, he was educationally operating at age seven; now he has nearly caught up with his peers. He no longer thinks he is "stupid", as the children in the mainstream school used to call him. He is proud of his achievements and feels that school is a safe place. He is flourishing. He still has to deal with the challenges that FASD presents, but the therapeutic residential school experience is giving him new coping strategies and supporting his learning in areas such as relationships and emotional regulation.*
>
> *And my worries that I was losing my son…totally unfounded. My son doesn't know that he is a "looked after child", he simply believes he is in the "right school". We are still very much a family, I am still very much a mum, family relationships have improved, and my son comes home most weekends. Weekends are now (mostly) enjoyable for us all.*
>
> (Judith, adoptive mother)

All of these options can provide smaller classes, teachers who are trained and experienced with pupils with additional support needs, and a peer group in which a child with difficulties will not stand out for the wrong reasons – because all the children face their own challenges. They are likely to provide a more nurturing environment where children are not defined by their differences, and their qualities and strengths in a wider range of areas are recognised and celebrated.

Unfortunately, the choice of school within the three categories is likely to be restricted, especially if you live outside of the Central Belt in Scotland, and the availability of places is limited.

> *Independent special schools will often have superior facilities and resources such as in-house therapists, and they will more often specialise in a condition. County (local authority) special schools can be a jack-of-all-trades, dealing with a wide range of conditions, and therapy provision can be scant (relying on visiting NHS professionals who will be severely overstretched).*

You need to investigate each school's pupil cohort. Are there some children of similar ability, even if they are different ages? (Special schools usually teach in ability groups rather than strict age groups.) Is there a good range of extracurricular activities?

Of course the price tag for the independent specialists is usually significantly higher, so choosing one can require you to prove that it is the only suitable provision through a stressful tribunal. And don't be swayed by a local authority telling you your child should go to mainstream [school]. It's easy to see this as a signal that everything will work out, and your child's needs are not as severe as you feared, but remember that mainstream is the default option for local authorities, and they are likely to have pound signs rather than your child's best interest front of mind.

(John, 2017, p.77)

(For organisations offering help and advice to parents of children with special needs, again see the section on Co-ordinated Support Plans, Chapter 6.)

Key points

- Your child does not need to start full-time school at four if you feel he isn't ready.
- Choosing the right school for your child means assessing how ready the staff are to learn from you about your child and how flexible they might be about accommodating his needs in a thoughtful way.
- There are a number of ways in which you and the school can support your child when he first starts school.
- For children with additional support needs, mainstream school may seem desirable but it may not be the best option. Special schools, special units and residential schools have the advantages of smaller classes, trained staff and a more nurturing environment.

5 Working with your child's school and teachers

We have said it before and we'll say it again: you are the expert on your child. But sometimes parents lack confidence when it comes to speaking with education professionals. Do bear in mind that, generally speaking, schools want to do the best for every child and are juggling complicated demands on what is available. In the interests of maintaining communication and relationships, try to hold onto this assumption and if you feel that your child's needs are not being met, be prepared to work together with school staff to find the best solution. The more informed you can be, the more confidence you will have. We hope that this chapter will be useful in helping you think about how to work with your child's school.

Interaction between home and school

School is a huge part of your child's life, and of course it impacts on how she feels about herself and everything she does. For adoptive parents, it can be a joy to see your son or daughter wake up in the mornings looking forward to the school day, having fun with their friends, mastering new skills, developing new interests and growing in confidence.

But if things are a struggle for your child at school, you are likely to bear the brunt of her feelings at home. Some adoptive parents report that their child has to make a huge effort at school all day to bottle up her feelings and cope with the stress of the classroom, school work, the playground and relationships with other children – only for her emotions to explode as soon as she gets to the safety of home.

She also has to cope with the power of the internet and social networking. These days, children as young as toddlers are watching content on tablets and mobile phones, with some people concerned about the possible long-term impact on their well-being. Many primary-school age children bring smartphones to school. (The effects of this – and especially the risks posed by social networking – are discussed at the end of Chapter 7.)

If the school environment is poor, with disruptive behaviour and negative relationships, this can make any child feel unsafe and anxious, and of course the impact of this will be greater on some children than others. If your child does not feel included and respected, with her achievements and contributions being valued and celebrated, she will not be able to form the good relationships with her teachers and peers that are essential to her well-being and learning. A teacher who is sarcastic or shouts a lot in the classroom can adversely affect all the children in the class, but again, the impact may be greater on a more vulnerable child.

Parents often have to deal with the fall-out of an environment that is not right for their child at school. Sometimes a child can have angry and destructive meltdowns; at other times it might be tears and sleepless nights. Of course, there may well be anger, tears and sleepless nights for parents themselves in these situations.

For some children, it is the other way around – they seem fine at home, but they cannot manage their feelings, emotions and behaviour while they are in school.

All sorts of factors both in and out of school can affect a child's ability to learn and to manage at school. For example, adopted children might have a lot going on in their minds that their parents are unaware of, because the child doesn't talk about it. A child may be constantly thinking and worrying about the welfare of birth family members or contact with birth relatives; she may have unresolved anger and questions about her adoption; she may fear not being "good enough", or feel that she doesn't belong in her adoptive family.

Talk to your child to try and find out what is going on for her and if anything is worrying or frightening her, either related to school or anything else in her life. Find ways to help your child express what is going on for her. Discuss your concerns with teachers. Seek outside help if necessary, for example, from your post-adoption support worker. Perhaps your child might benefit from some sessions with a play therapist, drama or art therapist to help her express her feelings and worries. It's always better to try and address matters at an early stage rather than waiting for a crisis. Hopefully you will be able to discuss with your school how you can both support her through her difficulties and get her to a better place.

Finding some out-of-school activities that your child enjoys will help with her overall confidence and self-esteem, which will have knock-on effects in school too. If she can join a group like the Woodcraft Folk, Scouts, a cadet group, a dance class, sports club or band, for example, she may be able to have positive experiences and form new friendships there that will go some way to counteract negative experiences in the classroom and playground. If she can develop her skills and talents – and be respected within the group for it – this can help your child to feel better about herself, which will build her resilience.

Education planning for adopted children

Looked after children should all have some form of learning/education plan, to ensure that teachers and others come together to discuss their progress and what support they might need in terms of their education. This is to fulfil corporate parenting duties. In the case of adopted children, there is no statutory requirement for a formal education plan because they now have a parent/s who will keep track of their educational progress.

Schools and nurseries should plan and keep under review all pupils' learning and development – called Personal Learning Planning. Other types of plan are used in order to deliver and review any additional support your child needs in order for them to learn. You, as a parent, can ask for an assessment of your child's needs or the school may suggest it, either when you adopt a school-aged child or when your adopted child starts at a new school. School staff should work with you, your child and, where necessary, other professionals to plan to give your child the support she needs to do the best she can. Many local authorities use Staged Intervention, which aims to meet a child's needs at the earliest opportunity and with the least intrusive level of intervention. Sometimes they will suggest a particular type of plan, and at other times it might be a more informal agreement. Whatever is decided, it should establish ongoing regular reviews of your child's progress at school and planning for the future. How regularly meetings happen will be decided by the people at the review meetings, for example, it might be once a term or once a year. Meetings are likely to involve a member of the school staff (ideally with specialised knowledge), other teachers such as the child's class teacher, parent(s), and other professionals involved with the child. You may choose to invite, for example, your post-adoption support worker, at least at the beginning (see the comment below).

The Enquire Factsheet *Planning your Child's Support* provides a clear explanation of the different types of plans used (www.enquire.org.uk/publications/planning).

The meetings should look at all aspects of the child's need, using the SHANARRI well-being indicators, and also more specific upcoming activities, such as school trips, potentially sensitive curriculum topics, transitions, communication between home and school, and any other information, including things that the child finds difficult and where she would benefit from extra support. SHANARRI stands for:

- Safe
- Healthy
- Achieving
- Nurtured
- Active
- Respected
- Responsible
- Included

and is part of the GIRFEC framework. A straightforward explanation can be found in the Government leaflet, *Understanding Well-being: Considering the quality of children and young people's lives* (https://www.gov.scot/publications/getting-right-child-understanding-wellbeing-leaflet/pages/1/).

The meetings will decide on actions to be taken by the adults around the child to support her in or out of school, such as ways to help her cope with playtimes or lunchtimes and any special arrangements that might be needed for tests or exams. The meetings would also be a good time to discuss any initiatives funded by PEF or CECYPF and whether these would be of benefit to your child.

> *It is essential for a member of the post-adoption team to attend the first school planning meeting with you. It adds a professional voice to the meeting, not only focusing on an individual child but can also lead to wider discussions about how adopted children's needs are met within the school.*
>
> (Karen Wilkins, adoptive mother)

Pupil Equity Fund

The Pupil Equity Fund (PEF) is part of the Attainment Scotland Fund provided by Scottish Government. Head teachers decide how to spend it, but it must be on interventions and approaches targeted at closing the poverty-related attainment gap. Sometimes this may also benefit adopted children and head teachers have the discretion to include them, as long as this is not detrimental to the key group of children and young people who are not able to achieve their full potential due to poverty. Many schools see the value of implementing "whole-school" approaches so that certain groups of children are not stigmatised.

PEF is allocated according to the number of children in P1–S3 known to be eligible for free school meals. Scottish Government publishes these allocations annually, so you can identify how much your child's school has been allocated and you can ask how it is being used (see https://www.gov.scot/policies/schools/pupil-attainment/).

Do parents have a say about how PEF is used?

Not directly, but as with other aspects of school life, parents and carers should be kept informed by their school and have the chance to share their thoughts and ideas on how the money could be spent as part of school plans. The more you can build a relationship with your school, the more your voice will be listened to. This could be through the Parent Council/Forum, or it might be through other parent associations or discussion groups. Schools are encouraged to be collaborative and creative about the ways in which they work with families, carers, the third sector and others in the ways that they use the money. They are also expected to spend their allocation to benefit groups of children rather than individuals. This means that suggestions for broad impact strategies which can be built on, for example, whole-school attachment training, are more likely to be taken forward than support for an individual pupil. Education Scotland has published advice to schools on how to make best possible use of their funding (see https://education.gov.scot/improvement/self-evaluation/interventions-for-equity).

Care Experienced Children and Young People's Fund

The Care Experienced Children and Young People's Fund (CECYPF) was set up in 2018 and also comes from the Attainment Scotland Fund. The money is held by local authorities, jointly administered by the Chief Officers for education and social work, and is to be used to improve the attainment of care experienced children and young people in their area. The activities funded may be in or out of the school setting, but they must enhance a child's capacity or readiness to learn. Although the money is allocated according to the number of looked after children in the local authority, it is clearly stated in the Government guidance that the money is for the benefit of all care experienced children and young people, not just those currently in care (www.gov.scot/publications/care-experienced-children-and-young-people-fund-operational-guidance). There has been quite a lot of confusion reported about this, with some local authorities and schools assuming that this funding is only for looked after children. So far, a wide range of initiatives has been funded, including establishing virtual schools in 15 local authorities (in addition to the one already in operation in Aberdeen City). Further information is available in the Our Work/Education area of the CELCIS website and at CELCIS (2019).

> *I received £500 for art tuition from my local authority for my adopted daughter, Charlotte. She had to submit the request in her own words. Charlotte's art skills are pretty basic but her birth mum is very creative. So the extra tuition was to enhance her skills, to provide enjoyment (she loves all sensory experiences) and to give her a connection to her birth family. I had to send in receipts, photo evidence and written evidence.*

(Fiona, adoptive mother)

A more detailed explanation of how the PEF and CECYPF can be used for adopted children is available in the Adoption UK in Scotland Factsheet, *Education Funding Support for Adopted Children in School* (www.adoptionuk.org/factsheets-scotland).

Be proactive about communicating with the school

Primary schools tend to be better at regular home–school communication than secondary schools.

The most important way that you can work with your child's school is by sharing with them what you know about your child. You can give the school and teachers hugely important insights into what will work best for her. However, this does take a lot of time and energy on your part. Also, you will probably have to do the same at the start of every school year, as teachers change.

When your child joins a school, meet and get to know key support staff who will work with her, so that the school knows what the likely issues might be. Do this early on, before any problems arise.

From the start, ask the teacher or principal support for learning teacher if you can have regular meetings to discuss your child's progress. Regular meetings are a good idea even if things are going well, but of course the teacher may have other more pressing priorities if your child is doing fine. In this case, you might need to make it a shorter meeting or a check-in phone call instead. When times get tough, it helps if you've already built a relationship and you can all reflect on things that the child has been able to do well before.

Make a "profile" about your child, with her help. This can be a one-page document that describes what she likes, what she doesn't like, anything she might find particularly difficult and what might help, and so on. This can then be shared with all the teachers who are likely to come into contact with your child.

Arrange for the school to give you advance notice of any changes coming up in school that might affect your child.

It can be helpful for the school if you are able to tell them about anything coming up for your child at home that could potentially be upsetting – such as letterbox contact, face-to-face birth family contact – or if you have had to break bad news to the child.

Your child might not know or might not want to tell you about homework or what's coming up at school, but there may be electronic timetables that parents can access or children may be given a timetable and/or a home-school diary (a communication tool between parents and staff), so you can check.

> *From my point of view, it's important to be as open and honest as it's possible to be with the right people in school so they have a good understanding of the situation and you can support them in getting it right. Communication is key. If you sit back and don't say anything, they are not going to understand or be aware of the needs.*
>
> (Claire Hiorns, personal communication)

Many adoptive parents, who are new to all this, wonder how often they can go into school without being considered pushy or overprotective.

> *One thing we sometimes get from schools* [about adoptive parents] *is 'they are incredibly anxious and it's as though they think their child is the only one we've got', so one of the things we've been trying to help schools do is to place themselves in the shoes of an adoptive parent and understand where these anxieties are coming from. I think if the school get it right in terms of the relationship with the family and showing the parents that they have also got the child's best interests at heart and that they are listening, that is going to alleviate a lot of those anxieties. All the parents want to know is that their child is safe and that they are happy and making progress.*
>
> (Claire Hiorns, Cambridgeshire Virtual School, personal communication)

How much should you tell the school about your child's circumstances before you adopted them?

This is a very personal decision. Some information is obviously going to help your child's teachers to understand him or her better, but you will want to keep certain things back. Check with whom the information is going to be shared; it should be on a "need to know" basis.

> *I was at a meeting at a secondary* [school] *where parents wanted to share with the staff the extremes of what their child had been through. The teachers said, 'Wow, OK, no wonder he was a bit difficult in my class. If he has lived with that, I'm more prepared to deal with it and more willing to – not overlook it, but acknowledge where those behaviours are coming*

from.' So it can be extremely powerful – it's just whether or not parents feel comfortable.

(Helen Hoban, Head of Education, PAC-UK, personal communication)

Should parents ask their child before sharing information with teachers?

Rather than asking the question, it might be better to have a conversation and say, 'We think it's really important that your teachers understand some things in order to make sure they can keep you feeling safe at school'. If parents say, 'Here are some things that we think they might need to know, how do you feel?' or 'Pick the two things you think are most important', the child still gets some say in it but also the parent is still steering it. Even at secondary school I'm not sure how able some children would be to make that decision.

(Helen Hoban, Head of Education, PAC-UK, personal communication)

Managing trauma triggers and curriculum hotspots

If you know what triggers traumatic memories for your child, make the school aware of these things.

For example, if your child really struggles with loud noises, you may need to say: 'Because of something that happened in early life, sudden loud noises are a real problem for Jane so here are some strategies to help her cope'. Or: 'How can you as a school minimise the impact of the fire alarm? Can she have some earplugs in her pocket to use, and can staff be made aware that she can wear them, so she is not told off for it?'

When you are letting your child's teacher know that your child is adopted and what issues or behaviour might crop up, ask the teacher to discuss it with you if there is anything coming up in the curriculum that might be a difficult issue for your child.

There are many ways in which teachers can manage these situations in a supportive way, points out Claire Hiorns of Cambridgeshire Virtual School, who provides training for schools on how to support adopted children:

We talk about, where possible, adapting the content for the whole class so the whole class are still meeting the learning outcomes but they are not doing something different for one child, so that the child doesn't feel singled out.

If they are doing a topic with bringing in baby pictures, they can say, 'Bring in a picture of when you were younger,' which could mean three weeks ago. As for looking at family trees, it doesn't have to be a personal family tree; they could look at the family tree of a famous person, or they could look at presenting it differently so it's not just a tree, it's an orchard, so they are considering the complexities.

All of that needs to be discussed with the family and thought about in terms of the implications. The child might need a key adult with them. All the way through we talk about there's no "one size fits all", every child is different, every family is different, therefore, it's about having that communication and thinking about them as an individual and planning accordingly.

Groups for adoptive parents

You might feel very isolated as an adoptive parent. Other parents have formed social groups from prenatal classes and pre-school groups, and they might be difficult to break into. Some other parents can have very little understanding of adoption and avoid the parents of "misbehaving" children. If you can find other adoptive parents, foster carers and kinship carers, you will have a lot in common and may also be able to speak as one voice to the school about policies affecting your children, e.g. approaches to promoting positive behaviour and the CECYPF. Online groups can also be very supportive; you'll realise that you are not the only one having difficulties and learn from each other's experiences.

Supporting your child through transitions

Major transitions, such as the start of a new school year or moving to a new school, as well as more minor transitions such as moving from classroom to classroom or from school to home at the end of the day, can be challenging for many adopted children. When a child has had times in her life when she has felt unsure or unsafe and lacked a sense of a "secure base", a transition can trigger the anxiety and fear she has felt before.

Some transitions are a big leap for children and parents alike. You might be worried about how your child is going to cope in a new class or new school. You need, of course, to be accepting of her feelings about the upcoming changes and acknowledge that she may be feeling worried or scared – but also try to anticipate the positives and be excited about the change when you talk with her about it, so that you transmit positive feelings rather than your anxiety.

Strategies that might help when your child starts school or makes the transition to secondary school are outlined in Chapters 4 and 7.

The following suggestions can help with other types of transition:

- Ask the school to give you prior warning, for example, if there is going to be a substitute teacher or change of classroom, so that you prepare your child by talking it through with them in advance.

- If there's going to be a school trip, your child could take a "transitional object" with her (see next section, 'Separation anxiety'). Ask staff if the itinerary can be adapted to meet her needs, e.g. perhaps she could join the class for the daytime activities only, rather than staying overnight, or join a residential trip halfway through so she is not away for so long.

- You may be able to prepare your child for a trip or something like sports day by showing her photos or taking her to the actual place where she will be going.

- Ask the teacher if it's possible to provide your child with signs or a storyboard showing what the class will do and when – assembly, maths, reading, lunchtime, breaktime, etc.

- Have the school timetable or a visual representation of the school day in a prominent place at home, such as on the fridge, so your child can see what is going to happen day by day.

- A new school bag, new pencils, etc, may help your child to feel more positive about the change.

- If you can, get involved in the life of the school. For instance, if you help out on school trips and fundraising events, your child will see that you are working together with the school, and you will be able to be present at some events to help her feel more secure.

PAC-UK has useful tip sheets on the education resources page on its website, entitled Goodbyes and Transitions, and Reducing Trip Trauma (www.pac-uk.org/education-resources). Be aware that PAC-UK's education resources reflect education in England.

Separation anxiety

When a child is adopted, it can take some time to form attachments to new parents. Going to school for a full day can seem like a long time to be away from these recent attachment figures; she or he may wonder if their new parents will still be there at the end of the day or if they will forget them while they are out of sight. If necessary, it may be possible for your child to attend school part-time at first to mitigate these worries.

When a child has separation anxiety, giving them a "transitional object" to take to school can help. This is something they can keep with them to remind them of you, and to remind them that you are thinking of them during the day and will be there when school finishes. It could be any small item that evokes home, such as a small soft toy or a handkerchief with your scent on it.

If the teacher is another attachment figure for your child, it can also help for them to give the child something to take home (e.g. at weekends or holidays) to remind the child that the teacher is holding the child in mind; for example, some small item from the classroom for the child to "look after".

Having to peel a crying child away from you in order to make them go into school is a painful experience for both of you, especially when it goes on day after day. Ask the school what they suggest. Having a familiar member of staff or key person to greet your child in the playground when you arrive at school and perhaps take them into school before the rest of the children may make the parting a little easier.

Another way to alleviate separation anxiety is to volunteer within the school, even though you may well not be allowed to do so within your child's class:

> *The fact that you are on school premises some days means the child "holds you in mind" and feels you are part of their world when at school. Volunteering to read, help with the library or with the School Council are*

great opportunities not only to be around more at school but also to get to know the teaching and support staff. It helps with communication also.

(Karen Wilkins, adoptive mother)

When the school isn't getting it

Building trust and relationships and helping the child feel safe and accepted are the key to success at school as well as at home. But not all teachers and schools "get it", as this adoptive father explains:

They all love Tom and want to do their best for him but we've had to learn, as parents, how to parent this boy, which is something that most parents wouldn't recognise as parenting. But the school keeps saying to me: 'Are there any sanctions you use at home that work?' Well no, that's not how you deal with these children. I say, 'We don't have sanctions,' and they look at me aghast. They say, 'Well, what are the boundaries and discipline?' and I say, 'That's not how it works. It's all about relationships and building trust.' What matters is building the trust and we've done it, it's worked at home. I won't say it's easy – it's bloody difficult – but it's a different way of parenting and it has to be a different way of educating.

(Adoptive father, personal communication)

If you feel the school isn't listening to you sufficiently or you don't feel you are getting things across, sometimes it can help to have input from a professional who can speak to the staff and advocate on your child's behalf. Some parents ask their post-adoption social worker to attend meetings with them or even just a friend to be a neutral observer. Adoption UK in Scotland's Factsheet, *Preparing for a School Meeting* (www.adoptionuk.org/factsheets-scotland) contains practical advice. If things are very difficult, you might want to consider mediation. If your conflict with the school is about additional support for learning, your local authority must offer free, independent mediation services to try to resolve the disagreement.

If your local authority has a virtual school or virtual head teacher, they may be able to offer advice and guidance to you and your child's school. Your post-adoption support worker, educational consultancies or specific disability groups such as FASD Hub Scotland may be able to work in partnership with your child's school to address issues with your child or the school as a whole (see Useful resources and Appendix).

When others ask you and your child about adoption

You will want to discuss with your child how and what she shares with peers about her adoption story. This can, of course, be an issue for parents too, when other parents ask questions. You can talk to your child about why she may choose to keep her adoption and/or experiences "private" (but not "secret") and whom she can safely confide in at school. Children can be very open in their early years at primary school, and tell everybody they are adopted. Sometimes this information ends up being used in bullying in the later years and at high school. It can become a big issue.

I was picked on for being adopted at high school – but school didn't make any effort to deal with it. Their attitude was, just get on with it and deal with it. There was a lot of bullying. School talked the talk on supporting kids like me, but they didn't walk the walk.

(Maxine (age 16) – Adoption Week Scotland, Adopted Voices Conference November, 2018)

Helen Hoban, Head of Education at PAC-UK, suggests a few strategies for helping you and/or your child tackle difficult questions:

We do a training day for parents and one of the things we advise is practising with your child when that question comes up and owning their story. It's twofold: What do you want people to know? They might say they are happy for everybody to know everything. Then as parents you can hone that down slightly and say, 'OK, great that you want to be open, why don't we choose three things that you can tell? Maybe don't tell everybody everything yet but these are the three things that you share.'

And then you practise together over and over and they have got that to fall back on. The other thing is, what would you do if somebody came up and said, 'You're adopted, aren't you?' What are some general responses you could have?

> We use the acronym WISE up – walk away, ignore, share, educate more generally – quite often for the parents as much as for the child, if someone says 'What happened to your child?' or 'Adopted children have all been abused, haven't they, what's your kid's story?' Sadly adults do do this. (W.I.S.E Up workshops are offered by the adoption agency Scottish Adoption.)
>
> You can turn it around and instead of answering their question you can say, 'Yes, unfortunately quite a lot of children do go through difficult experiences before they are adopted – anyway, see you later, bye.'
>
> "Walk away and ignore" go against what we normally teach our children. We say don't ignore people, don't walk away when someone is talking to you, but in certain circumstances if someone is being rude or asking about something you don't want to talk about, it is OK to say, 'I don't want to talk about this, thank you' and walk away.
>
> We talk a lot about practising because a child can feel anxious about answering that question or feel caught on the spot. If they haven't had the chance to practise it at home in a comfortable environment with their parents, then they might not feel able to access that information in the heat of the moment.

Both children and adults are naturally curious but can sometimes ask intrusive questions that might leave you or your child feeling uncomfortable and awkward.

> I told some of my friends in P1 [about being adopted] 'cos I was quite proud of it then. But as I got older I didn't really want people to know, because they might not understand what that meant – or they might understand too much actually as they got older. Most of the people in my class still don't really understand what it means to be adopted…they don't understand the real meaning, or that it's permanent. And some kids used to ask me what it was like living in the home – when I've never lived in a children's home. They have all these ideas about it that are just wrong. Nobody at my new [high] school knows I'm adopted – I don't really want any of the kids who weren't at my primary to know. I don't want to get picked on for being different – I just want to be treated like a normal kid.
>
> (Rosy (S1 pupil) – Adoption Week Scotland, Adopted Voices conference, 2018)

> Let your child know who they can trust and approach in school if they have a burning question or need to discuss something in relation to their adoption that cannot wait until home time. Caution them against confiding in their peers. Friendships at primary school age can be volatile and inconsistent and information shared with a "friend" can sometimes be used against an adopted child. Children from the wider population are likely to have scant understanding of adoption – this is also true of many adults. Being singled out as the "adopted kid" is something adopted children are incredibly fearful of, as they generally want to fit in and be accepted. It is therefore critical to have a discussion with the child about who they can confide in within the school setting.
>
> We discussed this with the school's LAC [looked after children] *lead and shared our daughter's background with her (including information around having direct contact with birth siblings, which can be a trigger for her). It means that my daughter knows she can go and see Mrs S at any time and she will feel safe and listened to.*
>
> (Karen Wilkins, adoptive mother)

Homework

This sometimes causes real stress and conflict in adoptive families.

> I think as parents we all want to do what the school bids us and what others seem happy/more than able to manage, but then feel inadequate when our children hit the homework wall.
>
> (Karen Wilkins, adoptive mother)

If your child struggles to do the homework, even with your help, it may not be worth making a big issue out of it and possibly damaging the relationship you are building with them. If homework is an issue in your house, talk to the teacher about what support is available or could be put in place, such as a homework club. If it continues to be a problem, perhaps explain why you are not willing to force your child to complete homework if it's going to cause them a lot of stress.

Stuart Guest, head teacher of Colebourne Primary School in Birmingham and an adoptive father, is not a big believer in the value of homework in primary school and says he told his children's school that they would not necessarily be doing their homework. 'We don't let homework in our house damage relationships – the school can deal with it,' he says. He does make "homework time" as nice as possible for the children, with hot chocolate and biscuits, but doesn't allow it to become a big issue if the children really do not want to do it.

- Have set days and times for homework.
- Make it as pleasant a time and place as you can.
- Show you are willing to help.
- Think of something positive for your child for when she has done it, such as playing a game together.
- If your child is refusing to do it, you might want to consider adopting Stuart Guest's approach – especially with older children. They will see the consequences of not doing homework coming from the school, rather than from you.

Adoptive mother Karen Wilkins says that while she sees homework as a good "habit" for children to form, it is also important to differentiate the home and school environment, and home should not feel like a classroom. Their school has homework club on a Tuesday lunchtime which children are free to attend if they have not finished their homework task at home. They have support from teachers within this group and can choose whether to attend or not. At home, she tries to make homework time something to do at the start of the weekend, to get it out of the way. But if it isn't completed within a 20-minute window, they put the books away and go and do something fun.

Homework should be an opportunity for connection and affirmation. If it isn't, stop and change to a task that enables you and your child to have a positive connection.

(Fiona, adoptive mother and teacher)

Safeguarding for adopted children

As an adoptive parent, you may want to be sure your child will not feature in school photos or reports of school events on the school website or in the press.

Check with the school about its photography/publicity policy and how this will impact on your child.

> While the school will have a policy to ensure your child's photo is not featured on the website, etc, there are other softer issues that may crop up, such as the child appearing in a school play and other parents recording the performance and putting it on social media. Our school has a "no recording" policy during any performance, but balances the needs of other parents who wish to have a recording of a performance by re-running a song or two from the play at the end of the show. Children who are not, for whatever reason, wanting to be part of this are asked to return to the classroom. This needs to be handled sensitively in order to avoid singling out any individual children.
>
> (Karen Wilkins, adoptive mother)

Obviously you will let the school know if you are concerned about the risk of your child's birth relatives attempting to find or contact your child. (If it's a pre-adoptive placement, schools may have received this information from social workers, but it's best to check.) If necessary, a safeguarding plan should be put in place. This would include the child only being handed over to you as the carer or a named person and may involve the use of a password. If you are going to be late to collect your child, notify the school as soon as you can so that they can ensure that she is with an appropriate person who knows with whom she can go home.

Each school has a designated teacher responsible for child protection and safeguarding (often the head teacher) and this teacher should also be responsible for any privacy concerns.

Cherry Newby is a former primary head teacher and now adoptive mother. The following advice (adapted for Scotland), comes from her blog post on how parents can work with the school to safeguard their child:

> As a head teacher, I had a number of adopted children in the school and often came up against these issues. As an adoptive parent, I have been on the other side of the fence, and have learnt how to approach schools to ensure that my child is as safe as possible when they are not with me. Here are my top tips.

Names

If your child has not yet been adopted then the school will have their birth surname on the records. This makes perfect sense for schools as officially the child's name hasn't been changed. However, from a parent's point of view, we don't want their birth name on all documents, books, etc. You may be able to ask that the child "be known as" your surname, and that this is written on all documents and books. You do need to discuss this with your social worker as there can be legal reasons why it is not advisable. Once the adoption order is granted their name can be changed formally.

Make sure that birth family details are deleted from a school's database (if the school ever had this information), once the adoption order has been granted. There have been incidents of schools inadvertently contacting birth parents because their details had not been removed.

Websites/blogs

It is unusual to find a school that does not have a website containing all sorts of information, blogs and photos. The concern here is how to keep your child's photo off the website or blog. This is a pretty easy fix. All schools should ask you to complete a data protection form which allows you to give, or refuse, permission for photos. Schools are generally good at checking these forms but it is always worth checking the website on occasions in case a photo slips through (this could be because it's a whole-school photo or class photo), in which case a gentle reminder to the school office will rectify it immediately. However, it can lead to children being excluded from activities because schools think photo control will be too difficult.

Newsletters

This was a surprise one to me as a parent, but when my daughter won a prize her name was put onto the newsletter as her full name. Admittedly it was her adopted surname but I was uncomfortable about having any child's full name on a newsletter, so I spoke with the school who agreed and amended their policy so only the first name, or first name and initial of their surname was published.

Use the key word!

Sometimes, just sometimes, you will run into something that the class teacher can't (or won't) sort out or understand. So at this point, your best plan of action is to ask for a meeting with the head teacher and, when questioned about why you need a meeting, mention the key words: "safeguarding issues". This will get you in to see the head and will solve the problems quickly. However, you should use this strategy only when you really need to, otherwise it can damage your relationship with the class teacher if they don't feel trusted.

Lock-out

My final piece of advice is something I call "lock out". I came up with this in my first year as a Head when a birth parent was known to be phoning schools in the local area to try to identify which school their child attended. We introduced a "lock out" policy. Essentially this meant that the adoptive parents gave the school a list of people who might call the school (sometimes including social workers) and whom we could talk to about their child. If anyone else called, the office staff were instructed to say that there was no child by that name at the school and to immediately phone the adoptive parent.

Schools can be difficult places to negotiate and sometimes I find myself thinking 'How did this happen?' or 'Didn't they think?' It's at times like this that I take a step back and remember that schools and teachers are just people too, and mistakes do happen – it's what happens after the mistake has been pointed out that is important, and educating the school or teacher on the issues that can arise so that these mistakes aren't repeated in the future.

(Newby, 2016)

Glow – Digital Learning for Scotland

Glow is the national online service used in schools. It is a learning environment that provides learners (aged 3–18) and educators access to digital tools and resources for learning and teaching across the whole curriculum (www.glowconnect.org.uk). It is not an open system – only learners and adults who require access in relation to their teaching/support role have Glow accounts and they will have been Disclosure Scotland checked. However, an important feature of Glow is that it is impossible to be anonymous. All users have an email address as their username. When learners move on to using direct emailing, the address list helps them to identify the right person with whom they wish to communicate (the John Smith in P3 at their school rather than the S5 John Smith in a distant high school). They can check that contact they receive is from someone they know before opening it. There is also filtering of all email so that obviously abusive, profane or inappropriate content will not reach Glow recipients.

So Glow is designed to support collaboration between learners and schools within a local authority and across Scotland, and email addresses should only be visible to other Glow users who are teachers, support staff, learners and staff from national bodies. However, during the Covid-19 lockdown, when learners were using this system from home, weaknesses were detected. Using the address book as detailed above, all children (or anyone with access to the child's log in details/machine) could search for any other children in Scotland who attend a primary or secondary school, access their individual record (full name and school), and email/chat with them. This was obviously a safeguarding risk for adopted children and those in other care settings. As a result of Adoption UK in Scotland highlighting this, children's names are now only searchable to teachers (or other adults permitted to use the system), and children can only search for teachers' direct contact details. If you wish, your child can also be made ex-directory/hidden from staff and teachers' searches too. You should arrange this directly with the school.

Key points

- If you can, have regular meetings with key people at your child's school.
- The school might set up an educational support plan for your child so they can keep tabs on her well-being and progress.
- Make a "profile" of your child, with your child's help, so that all school staff will be aware of important things about her.
- Communicating with the school takes effort but it can help to ensure they understand your child's possible issues and triggers, make adjustments and ease him or her through transitions.
- If problems arise, having pre-existing good relationships can be invaluable.

6 Rights, additional support needs, exclusion and alternative provision

Admissions

Local authorities are obliged to offer every child a school place, and this is usually at the catchment school for their home address. However, if you want to choose another school, you have a right to request a place in any school in Scotland that is run by a local authority. You can also request a place at an independent or grant-aided special school in Scotland, or a school in England, Wales, Northern Ireland or outwith the UK that provides support wholly or mainly for children with additional support needs.

Apart from when your request is to a school outside the UK, the local authority has a duty to comply with your request, although not to provide your child with transport as they do with your catchment school. However, there are a number of reasons why they can refuse, for example, accepting your child would cause them to have to create an additional class. If you wish to make a placing request, talk to the school and the relevant local authority first. Most local authorities then have a standard form for you to complete. The more difficulty you anticipate in getting your request granted, the more you need to be very clear about why the school you are asking for will meet your child's needs whereas the catchment school would not.

You have a right to appeal if your request isn't granted (see www.mygov.scot/appeal-a-school-place-request). You can talk to your local authority first to ensure that they were aware of all the reasons for your request. If that doesn't help, you will need to make a formal appeal using your council's procedure. Appeals will usually require you to present your case in writing and also in person. This can be quite intimidating, and you should prepare thoroughly and consider taking someone with you to support you. If you are not successful at this hearing there is a further route of appeal via the Education Appeal Committee and beyond this to a Sheriff. The Enquire *Parents' Guide* (see Useful resources) and Factsheet *School Placements* (www.enquire.org.uk/publications/school-placements) provide more detailed information on choosing a school, making a placing request and making an appeal.

Your local authority will have information on its web page with advice and guidance on how to apply for a school place in your area and how to contact those responsible for the admission process. (See Chapter 4 on 'Choosing a school'.)

School inspection reports are available on the Education Scotland website (via www.education.gov.scot/parentzone/find-a-school) and detailed information on attainment, attendance, pupil characteristics and pupil/teacher numbers are recorded on the School Information Dashboard (www.education.gov.scot/parentzone/my-school/school-information-dashboard).

Additional Support Needs (ASN)

If a child is adopted when very young, it is rarely easy to predict what needs or difficulties might emerge as he grows. ASN and disabilities – e.g. learning difficulty, attachment disorder, FASD, autism – are not always obvious at the time of the adoption but may become apparent later on when he starts school or sometimes only when it becomes clear that your child cannot cope with the increased complexity of functioning in a secondary school.

Disabled children

Schools have to make "reasonable adjustments" for disabled children. These can include:

- changes to physical features, e.g. adding a ramp;
- changes to how learners are assessed;
- providing extra support and aids, e.g. specialist teachers or equipment.

Useful resources can be found at:

- Children's Health Scotland (www.childrenshealthscotland.org);

- Contact: for families with disabled children (www.contact.org.uk) – UK-wide but has a good range of Scottish information;
- Council for Disabled Children (www.councilfordisabledchildren.org.uk) – contains a list of support organisations in Scotland, although many of their other resources are England specific.

There is detailed Government guidance on supporting disabled children in all spheres of life (see www.gov.scot/publications/supporting-disabled-children-young-people-and-their-families).

Co-ordinated support plans

The general principle behind co-ordinated support plans (CSPs) is that they are a legally binding process to ensure the implementation of additional support for children aged 3–18 in school (including pre-school) education. Children must meet all the following criteria to qualify for a CSP. Their ASN must:

- significantly impact on their education;
- arise from complex or multiple factors;
- be likely to last for more than one year;
- require a high level of support from education and services outside education such as social work or health.

The CSP sets out what the objectives for the child are, how they will be supported to meet those objectives and who has what role. Each agency then has a legal duty to provide that support. The plan must be reviewed every 12 months. A child can only have a CSP if they are in school education (including pre-school) supplied by a local authority.

If you have arranged for your child to attend an independent or grant-aided school or you home educate, you can request your local authority to find out whether your child needs a CSP, but the local authority is not legally obliged to agree to your request.

Obtaining a CSP for your child is not an easy process. They are uncommon in mainstream schools and local authorities tend to be extremely resistant to children having them. Enquire produces a detailed Factsheet, *Co-ordinated Support Plans* (www.enquire.org.uk/publications/csps) and there is statutory guidance.[1] The National Autistic Society also produces very comprehensive and straightforward information (see https://bit.ly/2UjTNS2).

Creating a CSP

- You make a request directly to your local authority or through your child's school/nursery in a form that can be kept for future reference, e.g. letter or video.

- The local authority has eight weeks (16 if you make your request during the summer holiday period) to let you know whether they will accept your request.

- Your local authority has 16 weeks to assess whether your child needs a CSP. If they do decide your child needs one, they must also produce the completed plan within this time.

- Once notified that your child needs a CSP, you have the right to ask the local authority for a particular assessment of your child's needs, if you think it is needed.

The CSP must contain certain information, including the additional support your child needs, who will provide the support, the school or nursery your child attends and a review timetable.

If your child does not meet the CSP threshold (which is quite high), he or she will continue to be given additional support for learning (ASL) in school.

Disagreeing with a decision

You can challenge your local authority about:

- their decision to not carry out an assessment;
- their decision to not create a CSP;
- failure to deliver the support set out in the CSP;
- failure to meet timescales for informing you of decisions, preparing or reviewing the CSP.

---

[1] *The Supporting Children's Learning Code of Practice* (3rd edition). Statutory Guidance for the Education (Additional Support for Learning) (Scotland) Act 2004 (as amended).

If you can't resolve the problem with your local authority, you can appeal to the First Tier Tribunal for Scotland Health and Education Chamber (formerly the Additional Support Needs Tribunal for Scotland) (www.healthandeducationchamber.scot/additional-support-needs/53). You only have two months to make an appeal, so you might need to do so at the same time as trying to resolve the problem directly with the local authority. Mediation services are available.

CSP system failings

On the ground, the CSP process does not always work as well as it should. Many parents feel that it is a battle to get this plan for their child and a very isolating experience. Even when a need for a CSP has been agreed, actually getting the process carried out properly can be very difficult.

The recent Government review into how additional support for learning works in practice (Scottish Government, 2020) identified a number of issues related to CSPs:

- *impact of austerity creating a risk of need being defined by the support provided;*
- *widespread misunderstanding: the CSP being regarded as an outcome in itself rather than a tool for effective planning;*
- *CSP being viewed as a gateway to access support, when the support identified within other plans had not been delivered;*
- *support and interventions agreed as part of the CSP not being fully implemented or reviewed robustly;*
- *parents/carers feeling frustration, anxiety, disappointment and weariness with the system;*
- *a lengthy and demanding appeals process.*

It was recommended that the CSP system be reviewed, taking account of these findings. Of particular relevance to adoptive families are the directions that:

> *the interaction between CSPs, Child's Plans and GIRFEC be clarified*

and

the relationship between education and partners in health, social work and other agencies be considered to identify where re-alignment is needed in the preparation and delivery of support.

There are many support groups, both in person and online/Facebook groups, of parents who are going through similar things – linking up with other parents is often really supportive. For example, the FASD Hub Scotland Peer Support Group is a private (secure) Facebook group and an online support community for people with FASD and those who care for them; Home For Good – Scotland is a Christian adopters/foster carers support group; and Scottish Adoption has an online teenage adopted person community called Teen Talk.

You can also:

- Consult your local authority's virtual school head (VSH) (if they have one).
- Contact Enquire – the Scottish advice service for additional support for learning.
- Contact Children's Health Scotland.

Applying for a CSP: two families' experiences

In primary school

We adopted our son when he was nine months old and he is now seven with a triple diagnosis of FASD, ASD and ADHD. When he started nursery, we quickly realised that his behaviour had a neurological root – that he was not just wilful or our parenting faulty. We applied for a CSP to meet his needs and ensure that school staff understood his needs and actions through a neurological rather than a behavioural lens. Shifting their perspective from "won't" to "can't", along with building a strong team of professionals around him has been fundamental in his successful transition to P1 and then P2. Principally, however, we applied for the CSP because we felt it protected him from school exclusion on the grounds of bad behaviour. Our son currently has support from outside agencies including CAMHS, Speech and Language therapy, ASL support from outside school and Occupational Therapy.

Applying for a CSP was a lengthy and extremely frustrating process. I started in his final year at nursery and it took more than a year of numerous phone calls, emailing numerous documents, involvement of the CAMHS clinical psychologist and threats of escalation beyond local authority level to receive a draft CSP – which was inadequate and out of date. By the end of P2, we had still not had the meeting to discuss how the draft CSP should be amended. In the meantime, the head teacher retired, and her replacement is much more knowledgeable and understanding and has implemented appropriate support for our son. So for the moment, we have paused this particular battle. As parents of a child with complex needs, we have many to fight! But if we feel that his support is not meeting his needs, updating the CSP will be moved off the back burner.

(Ailsa, adoptive mother)

In secondary school

Our experience of trying to get a CSP has been very frustrating. My daughter Sophie had an increasingly difficult progression through primary school where there was very little understanding of the underlying causes of her behaviour. The instigation of an IEP seemed only to result in stigmatisation of Sophie by staff and other pupils, and erosion of her self-esteem. Although Sophie had an enhanced transition to high school, they were keen that she should start with a "clean slate", and her teachers were given no information about her background or difficulties. She managed for about five weeks before things fell apart. Again, the school's focus was all about managing her behaviour, not seeking to identify and address the reasons for it and she was excluded during S2. Even though the school withdrew the exclusion, Sophie didn't feel able to return to school and hasn't been back since. We sought support for her with the Partners in Advocacy organisation, who felt that she should have a CSP. They wrote to our local authority and it was agreed. Their educational psychologist, asked to draw up the CSP, questioned if it was required as Sophie was engaging with the Out of School SEAL (Social and Emotional Aspects of Learning) team and in her opinion 'doing OK'. This did not address our concerns and those of occupational therapy, CAMHS and social services, and Sophie was still struggling with multiple issues although she had no formal diagnosis or visible disability. Since then we seem to be in stalemate. There have been several meetings, with actions agreed but never carried out. Sophie has lost all faith in the process and only attends meetings under protest and no longer engages with them. I am completely frustrated and because we live in an isolated rural area, there is no alternative school or local authority.

(Lewis, adoptive father)

Exclusion

Here are the facts about exclusion.

The head teacher and teachers at a child's school may feel the behaviour or problems a child is presenting are unacceptable. They may, therefore, decide to exclude the child. This is normally for very dangerous behaviour or a serious specific incident.

But the Government's most recent policy guidance makes it clear that exclusion should only be used as a last resort. All the factors and circumstances surrounding the incident leading to the exclusion should be considered as well as the purpose of the exclusion and the impact on the child or young person.

> *Where exclusion is used it should be a short-term measure with the aim of improving outcomes. It should enable further planning and assessment and provide an opportunity for reflection for both the child or young person and staff involved. Relationship-based approaches, such as solution oriented or restorative approaches, should be used to guide and support a child or young person's return to school.*
>
> (Scottish Government, June 2017c, p.7)

This guidance also makes specific reference to adopted children as having the same needs as when they were looked after and identifies how exclusion can be very damaging for them (p.29).

There are two kinds of exclusion: **temporary** and **removal from the register**.

Temporary exclusion (suspension)

This is an exclusion for a set period of time. The length of time for exclusions is not defined in legislation but it should be as short as possible. The power to exclude a child from school actually rests with the local authority, but they delegate that power to the senior management team within a school, and for some groups of children, for example, those with additional support needs, directly to the head teacher. The local authority remains responsible for a child's education while they are excluded and parents are expected to co-operate with any arrangements for this.

Removal from the register

This permanent exclusion is extremely rare in Scotland, with only three occurring in the most recent figures (2019). Everything possible should be considered to avoid such a situation, and the local authority remains responsible for children's continuing education. Educational provision with appropriate support should be put in place during any interim period before a child transfers to a new establishment.

Alternatives to exclusion

Exclusion has been identified as being very detrimental to children's well-being and attainment and often impacts more on children who are already disadvantaged in some way. So exclusion should only be used as a last resort, with promotion of prevention, early intervention and staged intervention as described in Scottish Government guidance (2017c). Some alternatives to exclusion may include the use of:

- **a safe or nurturing space** for a short time. This should not be punitive or cause additional distress, and should only be used if it is part of the agreed plan for that individual. For example, it is recognised that this child needs time in a non-stimulating area in order to regulate;

- **flexible packages**, the use of individualised, planned packages of support that may include time in onsite school support and offsite support "centres", including community learning, home education, social work and third sector interventions. These need to be carefully negotiated, recorded and monitored;

- **hosting or managed moves**, a strategy that some local authorities use to allow a child to move to a different school within the same local authority where they might be better supported and/or benefit from a "fresh start". The child remains on the register of the original school for a trial period, but then transfers to the host school if everyone is satisfied that the arrangement is working well. It is important that there is careful assessment, planning and monitoring of these arrangements, and that parents and children are involved in the decisions. It should not be a means of passing the "problem" child around.

Our son was excluded from primary school several times during P6 and 7. Individual teachers and support for learning teachers had tried really hard to work with us to support his needs in school, but ultimately the head teacher was only interested in quick fixes. I was called into school every day to address something that had happened. At the point where the head teacher was threatening permanent exclusion and we were drafting an official complaint to the Chief Education Officer, a hosting arrangement with a nearby school was proposed. It was a much smaller, Catholic school, but what made the difference was their attitude. The head teacher greeted us with, 'This must be so upsetting for you. You must be so worried about your son.' They understood his needs and were flexible, he felt safe there. We were never called into school again.

(Kirsty, adoptive mother)

Scotland does not have Pupil Referral Units as the other nations in the UK do. There is a very small number of special schools (supporting around one per cent of the pupil population), but children and young people identified as "unable" to continue in mainstream classes in Scotland are most often educated in "inclusion/special units" or "inclusion/special bases" situated in mainstream schools and/or supported by their mainstream or special school on individualised education or vocational programmes. These can be very helpful, but it is important that children are supported in forming good relationships with their peers and don't feel stigmatised.

Unofficial exclusions

There is still some concern that the Government's figures for official school exclusions do not give the full picture, with "unofficial" exclusions and children in alternative provision and allegedly "elective" home education not being fully accounted for. While unofficial practices such as reduced timetables and sending children home early are occurring less frequently today than they may have done previously, anecdotal evidence, case histories and third sector reports confirm that they are still happening (McCluskey *et al*, 2019).

The most recent Government guidance clearly states that:

> ...all exclusions from school must be formally recorded. Children and young people must not be sent home on an "informal exclusion" or sent home to "cool off".

(Scottish Government, 2017c, p.25)

Adoption UK carried out a survey of adoptive parents in 2017, asking about their experiences of their children being excluded from school on a temporary or permanent basis. The charity continues to call on all the UK Governments to collect and analyse exclusion and performance statistics for adopted children, as they do for other cohorts.

The results from Scottish respondents indicated that adopted children were six times more likely to be temporarily excluded from school than their peers, and one-fifth (20 per cent) of these were only in P1 or P2 when they received their first temporary exclusion.

Official Government statistics show that looked after and ASN children are more likely to receive exclusions than their classmates. Adopted children share many of the same issues as looked after children and are overly represented within the ASN cohort. But despite this, official figures for adopted children being excluded are not currently collected and analysed by Scottish Government.

Adoption UK's self-selecting survey is indicative, rather than scientific, yet raises serious concerns that adopted children are more likely to be excluded than their classmates.

Becky White, Adoption UK's schools development officer[1] and the author of a report into the survey results, said:

> *The comparatively high number of exclusions of very young adopted children is particularly disturbing. Many of these children will have only recently moved to their new adoptive families and are then experiencing significant disruptions to their education at a vulnerable point in their lives.*

> *Adoptive parents are the experts on their children. They're fully aware of the problems their children regularly face in school – but this survey reveals the shocking extent of these problems.*

---

[1] Now Becky Brooks, Education Policy Adviser

During the school year 2015/16, 21 per cent of adopted children in Scottish schools represented in the survey had been informally excluded from school on a temporary basis – meaning their "exclusion" was not officially recorded. Of children who had been officially temporarily excluded, one-quarter had been excluded five or more times that year.

Becky White continued:

> *The true extent of this problem is being masked because schools are regularly asking adoptive parents to take their children home and keep them out of school, without recording them as exclusions. More children were informally excluded in this way in 2015/16 than were formally excluded. We need to find better ways of improving the situation for children and teachers rather than relying on exclusions.*
>
> *The challenge for us now is in convincing education professionals that extra support is needed for adopted children from the start – instead of waiting until they are at crisis-point.*
>
> *A third of adopted children had changed school and 11 per cent of adopted children had been home educated because their needs were not being adequately met. Eight per cent of respondents said that their child's school advised them to voluntarily remove their child to another school.*

(Adoption UK Report, 2017 – Scottish figures presented, extracted from UK figures)

Alternative arrangements

A child still has a right to education when excluded. If it is only for a few days they may not receive any teaching, but the school may send them work to complete at home and return for marking. If they are out of school for longer, then alternative arrangements must be made. These might involve the use of technology or involvement with out-of-school teams.

The alternative arrangements offered to children who are excluded are often far from ideal.

> *Sophie was excluded in S2 and has never felt able to go back to school. Her re-integration into school is supposed to be supported by the Out of School SEAL* [Social and Emotional Aspects of Learning] *team, but in spite of repeated requests and suggestions she has never had an assessment of her*

needs and has not received any therapeutic work. It's just about behaviour modification with no understanding of the reasons why she finds school so difficult. She is not receiving any education and I feel they have given up on re-integrating her into school. She just goes on placements to charity shops and things like that. It's just a baby-sitting service until she can leave school in six months' time.

(Lewis, adoptive father)

If you want to challenge your child's exclusion

If your child is excluded, the school must tell you on the day of the exclusion and check that it is safe to send your child home or ask you to come and collect them. They must write to you within eight days to tell you the reason your child was excluded and arrange a meeting to discuss the exclusion within seven days. They must also tell you how to appeal the exclusion.

You (or your child) have the right to appeal to your local authority's Education Appeals Committee. There is no deadline, but it's best to try and resolve the situation quickly. If you disagree with the decision of the committee, you have 28 days from the date of the decision to appeal to the Sheriff Court.

It is obviously very difficult for a child to return to school after a period of exclusion. This needs to be carefully managed to enable them to return to school in a positive way. It is good practice for there to be a meeting between you and the school, including your child, to discuss the plan, appropriate supports and expectations. However, it is not a legal requirement to have a pre-return meeting or to give guarantees or sign contracts of behaviour before your child is allowed to return to school.

Your local authority's policy on exclusion should be available online. Information is also provided in the Enquire *Parents' Guide* (see Useful resources) and Factsheet *Exclusion from School* (www.enquire.org.uk/publications/exclusion-school).

Moving your child to a new school: personal accounts

When school is not working out for your child, it can be a frustrating and upsetting experience for you all. If things have gone wrong, finding a school that will accept your child's difficulties and work with them can come as a huge relief.

The following blog was written by an adoptive parent whose attempts to work with her child's school were unsuccessful, but who found that her son thrived in his next school.

Unattached to school

Our son has been kicked out of school.

That is two-and-a-half years of almost constant struggle (and endless meetings) with the school reduced to just one line.

Two-and-a-half years of trying to get them to realise that his behaviour is not naughtiness and that it is controllable, two-and-a-half years of trying to make them understand his needs (which are quite typical of adopted and traumatised children) and the correct way to address them, two-and-a-half years of him suffering and consequently failing to get an education because of their inability to make him feel safe and calm.

Sadly, ultimately it boiled down to that one simple line and that is all that now matters for us.

The school tried – at times they tried very hard indeed – but their attempts were often misguided and sadly short lived. They would feel that they resolved one issue and another would raise its head and then they would simply give up. It has never felt that they were wanting to learn and to grow as a school; frustratingly it always felt like they were doing what was required to placate us – the frustrated, demanding parents. Without the belief that it was benefitting them too, I fear that their investment into it lacked any true conviction.

We never felt we had the understanding or the assistance of the SENCO (SLT) to fight our corner, or from the "pastoral support teacher" who barely seemed to even understand pastoral care – so it always felt like a battle we were fighting alone, and in hindsight we can see that it was one we were never destined to win.

The suggestion of finding him a "special school" was made regularly throughout the two-and-a-half years, yet nobody could tell us what kind of school he needed to be in or indeed where to find one.

Fortunately, we had started looking into alternatives and had found a school that seemed to offer an amazingly therapeutic approach within reasonable distance of where we lived and which does indeed put the special needs of its children first and foremost.

However, we were yet to introduce ourselves to the school or indeed apply for admission for our son, when on the last day of term the old school informed us that our son was no longer welcome there.

Thankfully the school we had found has been incredibly understanding and has accepted him pretty much immediately as they could see that it was a critical situation.

It's very early days and we are fully aware that we are in a "honeymoon period"; however, we are full of hope as so far things have been amazing. Our son is clearly at ease and comfortable in an environment that is welcoming and inclusive of his emotional needs.

They have not witnessed one issue so far and have said that his behaviour has been exemplary, and for the first time in a long while he is concentrating on work and he is actually achieving.

It is a total turnaround.

He is the same child, we are the same parents, parenting in the same way that we always have – yet the old school just couldn't accept that THEY were failing him and creating the environment that was so difficult for him to function in.

Our son is not a bad child; in fact, family and friends around us are shocked when we share the issues that the school have been facing as they know a child who is nothing like the one the school knows.

Even if it is just a "honeymoon period" which comes to an end and the new school is subjected to the behaviour that the previous school struggled so deeply with, we know that they will still not see him as a bad boy and, just like we have learnt to do at home, they will see that they are doing something wrong and they will address the situation accordingly.

Isn't that what ALL schools should be doing?

(Reproduced with permission of We Are Family (2017), https://bit.ly/2IssAKz)

Moving your child to a different school can be a worrying time as you wonder if you have made the right choice. How will they cope with the transition? Will they thrive? But a move to a new school can be transformative, as this mother found when her son, who has FASD, moved to a specialist school.

The following blog is reproduced with permission from the adoptive parent who wrote it.

The same child shines when seen through a different prism

Our guy seems to learn in leaps. It's never a steady upward curve for him. He plateaus and then without any seeming rhyme or reason to it, he jumps up to the next level. Each time this happens, he falls back in other areas. Perhaps foolishly, each time it happens, we allow ourselves to be hit hard by the regression.

We are in one of those times. Our home environment is suffering. Our pre-teen son is increasingly armed with new vocabulary and new attitude, fuelled by a new edginess in what he is watching on YouTube. Social pressures at school are causing him great distress. He is getting less physical activity now that he is at a new school. His walks to and from school and his after-school activities have been replaced with time spent in a taxi. He is out of the house and "on" from 8:00 am until 4:00 pm. It's a long day for him.

When I snuck away to write this blog, I was feeling down. I was thinking of the rough morning we just had (diverted eventually by a walk along a river). I was still smarting from the rough night we had last night (diverted only by nearly two hours in a pool) and the string of other rough nights and rough mornings we have had lately. The mess of the house. Work stresses. The fact that this morning we rushed out of the house after a meltdown, in survival mode, and I haven't had a shower. Again. Yes, when I started writing I wasn't in a great mood.

Then I remembered that a school report arrived yesterday. I stepped away from the computer to have a read. Page by page, my mood lightened. Yes! It hit me. Our son may be regressing at home, but at school he is progressing in leaps and bounds. Once again, I am amazed at the difference it is making now that he is in a specialist setting.

Last year we were so crushed by our son's report card, we never let him see it. In contrast, this time I told him I had his school report and wanted to show him. He groaned and visibly moved away from me, alarmed and ready to bolt. I put my hand on his back and said, 'No, wait – it's excellent. Listen.' And we skimmed his in-depth report together. He became more and more excited. After one especially positive comment, he whispered with utmost pride, 'Maybe I should get a new toy!' (proving that at least in some cases he can link some cause and some effect and also showing, perhaps not flatteringly, that as parents we have not been above pure bribery in the past).

In a school that understands not all kids' brains are wired the same, here's what these new teachers wrote:

- 'He's an eager and enthusiastic pupil'
- 'He has great ideas'
- 'He is not at all afraid of thinking outside of the box'
- 'His work benefits from his imagination'
- 'He makes his presence felt with his enthusiasm'
- 'He is keen to achieve good results'
- 'He is gaining greater confidence'
- 'He is a talented musician'
- 'He has an ability to create exciting and engaging musical performances'
- 'Polite'
- 'Very able'
- 'His attitude toward learning has been excellent'
- 'His confidence has improved'
- 'He has managed to express his colourful personality'
- 'I am delighted to have a pupil of such creativity and imagination at the school'

This is the same child who last year was chided in his report for "disruptive behaviour", for being "silly" and "distracting". The discouraged boy who was told he "needed to understand" his behaviour was "inappropriate". Who was marked down because he couldn't pay attention for "more than five minutes". The kid who we couldn't get out of the door to school because he was under so much pressure – this was happening as recently as five months ago.

I was especially struck by the comment on his current report from a science teacher. Last year, his science teacher commented on his final report that he repeatedly cried throughout the year when given instructions. Her reports were never positive, she saw only a problem student. Cue to this year, and here we are:

'He has worked hard in science lessons. He generally grasps new concepts quite quickly and enjoys the opportunities to work practically. He observes scientific experiences [experiments] *carefully. He follows instructions well and can work in a careful, systematic manner.'*

This is the same child.

He was so proud of this new report. We also talked about some of the comments that show his FASD is still affecting his ability to access education fully. He is starting to know these are areas where he always will have difficulty due to his FASD, areas where he will need to put strategies in place. When he read the bit about how he 'can easily become distracted and lose focus', he said: 'That happens sometimes, doesn't it?'

We acknowledged but brushed over the comments that 'he has yet to grasp cause and effect' and 'he must ensure he always listens carefully to an instruction so he knows what is expected of him'. We will continue to work with him to understand his FASD and also with his school to ensure they understand these challenges are not due to wilful disobedience, but because he will always, for life, need instructions broken down – preferably shown in a visual format, maybe even rehearsed. Whereas previously these sorts of comments dominated his reports, this time, these comments were decidedly in the minority.

The most touching moment was when he asked me to explain this comment, the one that made my mood brighten most: 'He needs to believe in himself because he already has gained the respect of many of his peers.' We went over that together, slowly. As its meaning sunk in, he glowed.

It doesn't mean what's happening at home is not real, not concerning. Of course, when things are flying and getting broken we must hear what those behaviours are saying and make necessary changes. A positive report doesn't make his social challenges any less difficult. Recently he told me, heartbreakingly, that he is being bullied every day. But seeing this report does help me believe that those educators around him can help him get past that hurdle too. He may be having trouble with one or two kids, but he also is "earning the respect of many". Can you imagine how wonderful that is for a kid who has been sidelined by too many of his peers throughout too much of his education up to this point? We are on a whole new level. The setbacks at home have been accompanied by great progress in other areas.

Remembering that makes it all a bit easier.

(SB-FASD, blogpost, 2017)

Home education

Your child has a right to an education, and once they reach school age it is your duty to provide that education. Although most parents fulfil this duty by sending their child to school, you can choose to do it in another way that does not involve sending your child to school, so long as you can provide an efficient education that is suitable for your child's age, ability and aptitude. Some parents decide that the best option for their child is to educate them at home, at least for a while. Sadly, some feel that they are left with no choice but to do this because school is not working for their child and they have run out of options.

You can home educate from the start if you like, but if you are taking your child out of a state school to home educate, you require the consent of your local authority (the local authority must not unreasonably withhold consent). So you should write to your local authority in advance of withdrawing your child from school, including a description of how you intend to provide an efficient and suitable education for them; for example, your ethos, the resources you intend to use, and how you will go about it. You are not obliged to give your reasons for your decision, but you may choose to do so and it may well be useful for the local authority to know why you have made this decision. You should receive a response within six weeks. If you decide to home educate from the start, you are not obliged to gain the consent of your local authority or to inform them of your decision, although they prefer to know and it is useful if you are involved with other agencies that this information is on record.

Local authorities do not have a duty to monitor home education on a day-to-day basis, but they do have a duty to intervene if they are not satisfied that you are providing an efficient and suitable education, whether or not your child has ever attended school. So your local authority is likely to ask you to supply information annually or contact you for a discussion or visit. There should be a quality improvement officer in the education department who will lead on home education. They are often the best person to keep in contact with.

Important considerations

If you home educate, your local authority has no legal duty to provide you with any support; for example, educational psychologist, co-ordinated support plan, or specialised tuition. You can ask for the services that would be provided in school and you may receive some assistance, but it is entirely at the discretion of the local authority.

When it comes to gaining qualifications, your child will have to be registered with an approved centre such as a school or college. It can be difficult to find a centre that will accept an "external candidate" and it may be very expensive. There is more detailed information available on the Schoolhouse website (see www.schoolhouse.org.uk/resources/faqs/exams-qualifications).

Flexi schooling

Flexi schooling is not the same as your child having a part-time timetable as part of an agreed programme of support for an identified need. However, you may feel that your child would benefit from a blended programme of home- and school-based education. You should discuss this with your school and local authority, but while they should consider your request, they are not obliged to grant it. Different local authorities have very different views.

You can link up with other local families in the same situation and perhaps share skills to teach your children, purchase services or go on trips and/or get involved in online communities of home-educating parents. There is, of course, an infinite amount of educational resources on the internet.

Additional resources

- Scottish Government Home Education Guidance (www.gov.scot/publications/home-education-guidance)
- www.homeeducationscotland.org.uk (Scotland specific)
- www.schoolhouse.org.uk (Scotland specific)
- www.educationalfreedom.org.uk/find-a-local-group (UK wide)
- www.bbc.co.uk/teach
- www.bbc.co.uk/bitesize

Facebook groups

- Home Education Scotland
- Home Educating in Forever Families (UK wide)
- Home Educating Families' Festival (HEFF) (UK wide)

Key points

- Requiring additional support in order to access learning should not be seen as a failure. View it as supplying what is necessary to give everyone equal access to education.
- Co-ordinated Support Plans (CSPs) are available for children and young people who have complex needs and require multi-agency support, who are being educated in state schools.
- The exclusion of adopted children is all too common, even at a very young age, highlighting the need for more specialist support.
- Children who struggle in one school can flourish in a different school or type of school.

7 Choosing and starting a new secondary school

Choosing a secondary school

Many of the questions you may need to ask when choosing a secondary school for your child overlap with those recommended for choosing a primary school (see Chapter 4). That said, several additional points relating to secondary education need to be considered when you are visiting schools to make your decision. Here are some more suggested questions.

Key questions for secondary schools

How does the school provide consistent key relationships for young people with attachment needs?

For example:
- form/class groups with tutors to check in at the start of the day;
- nurture time/group;
- non-teaching pastoral staff available throughout the day;
- learning mentors;
- for young people who receive one-to-one support, is support allocated to them (i.e. one consistent PSA/SLT) or to the subject (i.e. up to 10 PSA/SLTs)?

Is there a safe base for young people when they need to calm down or regulate?

- How does this work? Drop-in basis?

- Does the young person need specific permission to attend?
- How is it staffed?
- Are any drop-in spaces staffed consistently?

What is the school's ethos and culture?

- What language is used in school policies? For example, does it talk about "promoting positive behaviour" rather than "managing challenging behaviour", in line with Government guidance (Scottish Government, 2018).
- Does the school appear to follow a whole-school, restorative and supportive approach rather than a punitive one?
- How flexible does the school appear to be in providing opportunities for all young people?
- How does the school actively promote positive relationships in the classroom, social areas and wider community?
- How does the school hear their young people's voices and include them in decision-making?

What support is in place for young people who find unstructured times difficult?

For example:

- lunch club;
- drop-in base;
- structured activities;
- social skills groups.

How does the school provide structure and consistency?

For example:

- S1 in permanent base;
- lockers for young people's belongings;
- form tutor;

- approach to staff sickness and supply teachers;
- advance warning of timetable changes, building work, etc;
- timetable on the website so parents can prepare their young person at home.

How does the school support the P7 to S1 transition?

For example:

- extra visits for vulnerable young people;
- opportunities to see the school both empty and busy;
- maps and photos;
- summer club to get used to the school and key staff.

How does the school share information with parents?

For example:

- what equipment/kit is needed;
- homework/assessment timetable;
- web-based supported learning environment. Is this used by all staff? Do parents have log-ins?

How does the school support young people who find it difficult to manage their feelings?

For example:

- nurture groups;
- calm boxes/agreed activities such as listening to music, completing jigsaws, gardening;
- a calming zone within the school;
- mentoring;
- emotion regulation skills teaching and coaching;
- empathy from all staff.

How does the school manage curriculum hotspots, i.e. issues that might trigger your young person?

For example:

- liaise with parents about sex, alcohol, drugs, genetics education;
- pass on information about any particular triggers to members of teaching staff.

(Adapted from information originally developed by PAC-UK)

Transition to secondary school

A young person starting secondary school will meet and have to interact with many more young people, some of whom are likely to be familiar and friendly, but there will be many others who are unfamiliar and who appear scary, unpredictable, baffling or rejecting. Some adopted young people will still be developing the skills they need to get on with others. With new classmates come new pressures: making friends (who can be trusted?), keeping up with the rest of the class in lessons, holding your own, getting the jokes, looking right, wearing the right clothes, and keeping it together when you are feeling stressed. Instead of being the oldest year group in their primary school, they are suddenly the youngest – with many physically bigger, brasher young people in the years above them in school – which can be daunting.

They have to get to know lots of new teachers – ones who don't understand them yet – and they have several different teachers in the course of a day. There are new subjects, and previously familiar subjects are taught in different ways. There's a bigger school to find their way around, more classrooms to navigate, more noise and crowds to contend with in the school corridors, new subjects to get to grips with, more things to organise to take with them in the morning, different school rules to understand and remember, and more homework to do. There's a new route to school, which may be longer than before, and possibly the hurdle of travelling independently to school for the first time or using public transport when this has not previously been necessary.

All of these things are potential triggers for many adopted young people. They are likely to be completely out of their comfort zone for quite some time.

Helping your child make the transition

Some of the things schools can do are listed above, in 'Key questions for secondary schools.' As a parent, you could also consider the following:

- Ask your young person how she feels about going to secondary school and talk through any of the issues that are worrying her. If she tends to be uncommunicative, try going for a walk or a long drive somewhere together – that can sometimes help them to open up.
- Take her to visit the school at busy times and quiet times. Photos and/or a map of the school might help her understand the new layout.
- Take any opportunity to go to the Christmas fair, summer fair or any other events the school or Parent Forum puts on that are open to the public.
- If she is anxious about travelling to school by public transport, have several practice runs. Agree that you will do the home–school journey together a couple of times, then again with you following a short distance behind, then when she is confident let her do it by herself (or with a friend who will also be going to that school).
- Cultivate her friendships with young people who will be going to the same secondary school (and do the same with their parents!).
- Do role-plays with her of any situations that you think she might find difficult, such as introducing herself to a new person or asking someone else their name.
- Talk to her about why she might want to keep her adoption story private, and role-play how she might respond if it comes up.
- Ask her what she would like the teachers to know about her. If appropriate, involve her in putting together a profile that you can give to the school, or use what she has said when you are providing input into the Education Support Plan, if the school will be completing one of these for her.
- Be positive and enthusiastic about the new opportunities that the secondary school will offer – the range of sports, school facilities, the extracurricular clubs, bands, trips and other exciting things it has that primary school didn't.
- Help her decide how she is going to say thank you and goodbye to her favourite people from her old school and help her to, for example, make

cards and buy presents. Remind her that she can visit the school sometimes even after she has left.

- Remind her of ways in which she can keep in touch with some of her friends from her primary school if she will not be going to the same secondary school – such as going to Scouts or Guides, going swimming together or to the cinema at weekends.
- Plan a treat for the first weekend after she starts at the new school, so she has something nice to look forward to once she has got through that first week.
- Remind her of other times when she has been a bit nervous about going somewhere or doing something and has ended up really enjoying it.

What can help?

Many of the strategies to help adopted children in school discussed earlier in this book might seem more suited to primary schools than secondaries, but in fact they can be just as helpful for young people as for children.

A group of adopted young people were asked to look back on their school days and think about what could have made, or what did make, a difference. This is what they said:

- a separate room for exams and a separate room in school with a key adult you can go to;
- time to talk to the teachers when you need to, or when you need to calm down if you are upset;
- 'In secondary it was random teachers, like the chemistry teacher – a group of us could go and help him in break time to get away from the friendship dramas';
- extra help and extra time in exams;
- 'Drama helped me cope with everything I've been through.'

There are nurturing secondary schools out there but it's harder to get right by the very nature of secondary schools, says Helen Hoban from PAC-UK:

> *You need to find the developmental age of the young person you are working with and apply strategies that are appropriate for them.*
>
> *For example, when you would like a key person to meet with them, it might be that you have to find a way to make that work in a secondary school where it's so much bigger and young people say, 'I don't want to come and see you every morning, it's not cool.'*
>
> *How do you make it work in a way that supports the young person and feels achievable for the school? If the school thinks it's utterly impossible, they aren't going to implement anything. You could start with the idea that if each transition were to feel a little bit more supported for this young person, how could we do that? Often schools will then lead the conversation and say, 'Well, Miss Appleby* [the key person] *could just be in the corridor, just be around casually so the young person knows she's close by'. You reply, 'Oh yes, that could work, could you facilitate that?' And if this is realistic schools will say, 'Absolutely, we can make that work.' The idea is to support schools in recognising the wealth of knowledge and resources they already have and help with ways to use those resources. Ultimately, we all want the same thing, for the young person to feel safe in school.*
>
> *Whereas if you go in and say, 'She needs to have a PSA for every single transition and they must walk into the lesson with her,' that can sometimes feel a bit much. Ideally, we want schools to identify strategies that feel achievable leading from the questions and suggestions you make – then it is often better implemented and has more longevity and impact.*
>
> (Helen Hoban, Head of Education Service, PAC-UK, personal communication)

In secondary schools, young people are particularly aware of how they are viewed by their peers; they are keen to "blend in" and the last thing they want is to be singled out and treated differently. But at the same time, they do want teachers to understand.

One student comments:

> *So maybe don't give an adopted person extra attention but just be more aware, subtly, in the background, that they may need a chat afterwards or they may need to come and see you or they may exhibit challenging behaviour. I think a lot of adopted people, including myself, do exhibit challenging behaviour. They're not – well, I wasn't – trying to be deliberately difficult. I just couldn't help it. So try to see through the behaviour.*

In terms of potentially difficult curriculum issues and their impact on adopted students, another young woman said that teachers should ask the student how they feel rather than making assumptions:

Teachers shouldn't just assume it is an issue for them if they don't actually know. It would come across that the teacher is kicking a student out of the class when the student has no issue about what's going on in the class.

(Young people speaking as part of the Coram Adoptables schools project)

Exam pressure

A key difference between primary and secondary school is exams, and the importance that is placed on them. Exam pressure is stressful for most young people, but often constitutes an added burden for those who are adopted and have experienced trauma, and have attachment and neuro-developmental difficulties. Many adoptive parents, having seen how anxious and distressed their young people are at school, would unhesitatingly prioritise emotional well-being over good exam results, and it is difficult to see how you can gain the latter without the former.

A list to identify "high need" students for teachers

In secondary schools, there are many different members of staff and the teachers cannot know every young person personally. One way for a school to address this is to provide a "high need" list of students with photos and strategies, which can be given to all school staff so that they do not escalate a situation unwittingly because they do not know that young person's needs.

A student "passport"

Some schools provide a "passport" for certain adopted young people so that they can present it to different staff at the start of the lesson to tell them what is helpful or not helpful for them. For instance, a young person may feel extremely anxious about what is going on behind her and may be able to settle only when she is sitting at the back of the class and able to see the door.

Communicating with secondary school

For parents too, the transition to secondary school can take some adjustment. In primary school, there is one class teacher whom you can get to know and who can get to know you. When your young person starts secondary school, it means you will have a new type of relationship with the school. The quick exchanges you may have had with teachers and other staff at the primary school entrance will be a thing of the past.

If you want to speak to a teacher, SLT or other member of school staff, you need to get in touch with the school by phone or email to find out when they would be available. You may have to make an appointment to have a chat with them.

Every young person should have a learning plan, irrespective of whether they have additional support needs or not. This tends to be more formal in secondary school, and information about this should be available from your young person's school.

Home/school partnership

Scottish Government places a high priority on schools and parents working in partnership, recognising how a consistent approach between school and family supports learning and behaviour. Your young person's school should have information available on how it seeks to achieve this and to implement the ethos of GIRFEC. You and your child/young person should be included in planning for their learning, and in decision-making, on an equal footing with other people around the table, especially if your child/young person has been identified as needing additional support (for additional information on the rights of children and young people to be involved in decisions about their education, see: www.myrightsmysay.scot and www.reach.scot).

If there are communication difficulties

Adoption UK, FASD Hub Scotland and Enquire's helplines are able to offer advice to parents if communication has become difficult between them and their young person's school. Having a discussion with one of these organisations can help parents feel empowered to approach the school and reflect on how to have an effective conversation with school staff. The advisers can enable parents to identify the main issues and signpost them to the most relevant information to share with their child's/young person's school.

Parents might want to ask another professional from outside the school to support them in a meeting with the school.

For the celebrated author and adoptive mother Sally Donovan, the involvement of her adoption support social worker was critical when things were hanging in the balance for her son at secondary school.

How social worker and teacher combined to turn around my adopted son's education

One hot and sticky afternoon, almost exactly four years ago, Mr D and I and our social worker, our adopted son Jamie's teaching assistant, and several members of his secondary school's leadership team settled awkwardly around a big table in a small meeting room. It wasn't called a crisis meeting but, looking back, that's what it was.

My heart was going like the clappers because I knew there was so much at stake. We were on the verge of dreadfulness. This was the end of the first year in secondary school and things were unravelling, at school and at home. A child who had coped well at primary school was hyper-vigilant, unable to focus and behaving inappropriately. Our family was barely hanging on and school were wobbling over whether this was the right place for Jamie. It could all have gone disastrously.

It didn't go disastrously. Four years on and our son is at the same school, is about to sit GCSEs and has his prom suit hanging in his wardrobe. Our family has weathered some extraordinary times and is doing well. So what changed?

Looking back, there were two critical people at that meeting, without whom things could have turned out very differently.

Having a knowledgeable and skilled social worker alongside us shifted things considerably. He spoke with experience and knowledge about trauma, why it is present in some children, how it's not a choice, and why trying to threaten, train or exclude it away can make things worse.

He was able to suggest workable and flexible strategies that could be managed within the existing organisation, such as Jamie being able to leave the classroom, with no sanction, and seek safety in the student support centre.

Having a social worker say those things is far more powerful than a parent saying them. It sounds more like common sense and less like excuses.

Sat quietly at that table was the newly appointed head of year. She listened carefully and borrowed a book I had brought along (Inside I'm Hurting, by Louise Bombèr). The following term, she rang me from a course she was attending on supporting looked after and adopted children in school, run by Louise, to tell me how much sense it was all making and the ideas she had for supporting not just our adopted son, but many other children in school.

The stream of detentions and letters home dried up, further training was carried out, triggers were identified, regular meetings took place, nerves were held and relationships were built.

Relationships were built and that really is the heart of it.

Relationships have been built between Jamie and the staff supporting him and looking out for him and they've been built between school and home.

These relationships are grounded in mutual respect, kind honesty and continual adjustment and learning, and they have given us all the resilience to get through some difficult times.

Over these four years, the strategies and approaches put into place have improved feelings of safety and belonging. There hasn't been too much emphasis on academic learning, but rather on growing social and emotional skills while maintaining carefully chosen boundaries. Developing reflective skills has been particularly helpful, as has generally being made to feel welcome and valued at school. The learning is coming now, in great leaps, just ahead of the school finish line.

Raising children who see the world through the prism of trauma and shattered attachments can be a lonely and isolating business, particularly when the overwhelming narrative around schools can tend towards strong discipline, zero tolerance and no excuses. Our family have been lucky to have had the opportunity to build a relationship with a school prepared to work flexibly and with heart. This has enabled a young person who was dealt a tough hand to flourish.

There have been times along the way when success has been in the balance and that meeting four years ago was one of those times. What tipped the scales in the right direction was a skilled social worker and a school leadership willing to engage and to lead from the top.

(Donovan, 2016)

Adolescence and the teenage years

Much of what this guide covers in previous chapters applies to children and young people of all ages, up to starting in secondary school.

But secondary schools are very different from primary – and adolescents and teenagers are very different from younger children, so the road tends to get bumpier, if it hasn't already done so. The social pressures in adolescence are greater than those for younger children, there is more academic pressure, and young people's behaviour can become more extreme.

The brain of an adolescent will not be mature for some years yet, and extensive brain re-development is still taking place, especially in the areas that deal with controlling impulses and complex social behaviour.

The influence of a child's peer group grows stronger and stronger as he or she gets into the teenage years, and the influence of parents appears to wane. It's the age-old struggle as the adolescent tries to separate from their parents and become more independent, while parents can see that their child still needs some boundaries and protection (sometimes protection from themselves). Conflict is often a part of these years. Some schools have been using training packages such as the Solihull Approach and Raising Teens with Confidence to help teachers, parents and young people understand each other better and navigate these difficult years.

Don't give up trying to communicate with your teenager. You might find that, at times, teachers she likes and respects can get through to her better than you can, and other adults from outside the immediate family might be able to exert a positive influence.

In some adoptive families, these turbulent times are even more challenging. Children and teenagers who have experienced trauma can sometimes feel drawn to others who have too, or who have emotional and behavioural challenges of their own, leading them to get into friendship groups involved in antisocial and offending behaviour. They may self-medicate with alcohol and/or drugs to dull the pain of traumatic memories, loss, grief and unknown pasts.

The issue of child-to-parent violence (CPV) is becoming more widely recognised. In some adoptive families, children and adolescents are verbally abusive and controlling and even physically violent towards their parents; as they become bigger and stronger, their behaviour becomes even more difficult to cope with. Marriages and family relationships can collapse under the strain. Adoptions sometimes break down.

Adoption UK in Scotland offers training in a connective parenting approach based on the principles of non-violent resistance (NVR) for adoptive parents. You may find this helpful if you are in this distressing situation (for more information, contact Adoption UK in Scotland).

Some of the challenging issues facing teenagers (and their parents) are unfortunately well beyond the scope of this book. Don't forget that you can ask your local authority for post-adoption support for your child or family at any time – even if you've never asked for it before. This includes asking for an assessment of your needs.

Coming to terms with adoption

Adolescence is also a time when deeper questions start to be thought about in more abstract ways and questions of identity come to the fore. It's well known that the teenage years can be a time of existential angst and emotional intensity, but those who are adopted have even more complex feelings to grapple with than their peers.

> *In primary school I told everyone* [that I was adopted] *because I didn't really know what it meant, it was just something that made me "me". And just as someone will say, 'Oh, I live in London' I'd go, 'Oh, I live in London, I'm adopted' and people would go 'Oh, all right'. And then I hit sort of the teenage years and I thought, this is awful, I am so ashamed. No one understands. And due to that and, like, a number of different factors, I went slightly off the rails and made some poor choices. But no one really knew how it felt and no-one could really empathise. Particularly my friends, they completely didn't understand. So that wasn't great. But then when people began to realise that my challenging behaviour was to do with adoption*

and they gave me more time of day, it got a lot easier. So patience and the teachers listening really helped.

(Young woman, speaking as part of the Coram Adoptables schools project)

Adolescence is a time when curiosity about birth parents can increase and deepen, and sometimes become an unstoppable force. Parents need to give more detailed explanations to their child of why they were adopted and what their birth parents were like, and to make sure these explanations are not simplistic as they were in the early years, but appropriate to their greater understanding of human behaviour and social issues.

Some children and teenagers decide to search online for information or to find their birth family members – often without any support, mediation or safeguards and sometimes without the knowledge of their adoptive parents. This has been covered extensively elsewhere (e.g. in Eileen Fursland's 2013 book, *Facing up to Facebook: A survival guide for adoptive parents*) and again is beyond the scope of this book.

However, parents and teachers should perhaps reflect on how issues of wondering about, searching for – and sometimes also contacting, possibly in secret – birth parents and other relatives can become the focus of a child or teenager's thinking. There may be tragic and distressing events in the child's past which could be difficult for them to understand or come to terms with. This preoccupation can understandably interfere with a child or young person's ability to concentrate on schoolwork and homework.

> *Basically being adopted is hard. It's like, you have lots of stuff to think about and you might not sleep at night because you're thinking about it. You know, like also you want to meet your* [birth] *parents, but... I'm trying to meet my family but my mum's just drinking and stuff. So I'm like – well, I could put it off but eventually I want to meet her, I mean, she's my mum. And just imagine having eight children took away from her...so... I take pity on her, but also – well, there's not a nice way to say it, basically.*

(Young man, speaking as part of the Coram Adoptables schools project)

Peer pressure and bullying about adoption can intensify in these years. Friendships can be volatile and change overnight into enmity.

> *From a personal point of view, questions don't hurt. But jokes and rumours and speaking behind your back really do. So...if you have a problem, or if you*

> have a question, ask me – and if I don't want to speak about it, please respect that. But often I probably will. And if I do trust you with that information, it's because I've liked you or trusted you, so don't then exploit that.

(Young woman, speaking as part of the Coram Adoptables school project)

Sadly, some adopted children and young people are bullied in school or online, while others are simply left out – not included in games, invited to parties or to "hang out" with their peers. It goes without saying that these situations can be heartbreaking for children, teenagers and parents alike.

> At the age of seven I showed my best friend my life story book and we fell out a week later and she shouted at me: 'At least I'm not adopted!' That made me wary. I had a difficult start to secondary school. Friends didn't include me, they were nasty to me and I kept my feelings bottled up. When I did tell my mum I was moved to another form and I found a new group of friends, but I still didn't feel I fitted in. I still struggle to trust people but I've got more confidence since meeting my boyfriend.

(Cody, adopted young person speaking at Adoption UK conference, 2017)

> I was not bullied but I was isolated. The continual questions about my birth mother wore me down. The teacher didn't support me.

(Megan, adopted young person speaking at Adoption UK conference, 2017)

Report any bullying or abuse of your child to the school (keep a record of any abusive or offensive emails or messages and make sure your child or teenager knows not to reply). The school should be ready to deal with it robustly. It will have a policy on bullying – hold it to account. If the first person you report it to does not act, escalate it up the school management team. Since 2018, schools have been required to record and investigate complaints from pupils about bullying (see https://bit.ly/38FFXIg).

Gender-based violence is known to be a problem in Scottish society, and there is also evidence that young people, particularly girls, encounter physical, emotional and sexual violence. The Mentors in Violence Prevention (MVP) programme was introduced in Scottish schools in response to these issues. It is a peer mentoring programme that gives young people the chance to explore and challenge the attitudes, beliefs and cultural norms that underpin gender-based violence, bullying and other forms of violence. It addresses a range of behaviours, including name-calling, sexting,[1] controlling behaviour and harassment, and uses a "bystander" approach where individuals are not looked on as potential victims or perpetrators, but as empowered and active bystanders with the ability to support and challenge their peers in a safe way (see https://bit.ly/3kmSpbO).

Resources aimed at education staff on identifying, understanding and responding to harmful sexual behaviour involving children and young people are available on the Education Scotland National Improvement Hub (see https://bit.ly/2UeDZ32).

> **Useful organisations**
>
> Find out more about dealing with bullying through the following organisations.
>
> **respect*me*** (Scotland's Anti-Bullying Service) – resources for school staff, parents and carers as well as children and young people, including:
>
> - Policy through to Practice – Getting it Right. Anti-Bullying Policy Guidance for Schools and Children & Young People's Services;
> - Responding to Bullying – What are my options?
> - Bullying – What can I do? (YouTube video)
>
> www.respectme.org.uk
>
> **Respect for All** – the National Approach to Anti-Bullying for Scotland's Children and Young People: https://bit.ly/3kmqVmL
>
> **RSHP Scotland** – the national resource for relationships, sexual health and parenthood (RSHP) education for children and young people: www.rshp.scot
>
> **Anti-bullying Alliance** – www.anti-bullyingalliance.org.uk
>
> **Bullying UK** – www.bullying.co.uk/general-advice; tel: 0808 800 2222
>
> **Kidscape** – www.kidscape.org.uk; Parent Advice Line: 020 7823 5430

---

1 Sending sexually explicit texts or images to another person, using a mobile phone.

Social networking

The immense popularity of social networking with children, sometimes as early as primary school, is proving problematic for schools and parents alike. It has led to a rise in bullying, as well as less obvious emotional risks to the well-being of children and teenagers. The media generally, including online media, can have a damaging effect on girls' and boys' body image and self-esteem, leaving them feeling that they don't match up to the ideal of body shape and perceived beauty with which they are constantly bombarded. Looking at others' social media profiles can leave them feeling that everyone else is more popular and having a much better time than they are; the fact that everyone's social media is "curated" and will only show a small part of people's real lives can be hard to keep in mind. Children and young people can be left feeling disturbed by some of the violent and explicit videos they may see online. And online pornography, which children can stumble across unintentionally or find easily if they search for it, can produce skewed and unrealistic ideas about sex, relationships, and how partners would like to be treated.

Some schools are taking the step of banning mobile phones in school because of the distraction and aggravation caused by their use for social networking during class. Conversely, some high schools assume all pupils will have smartphones and expect them to be used as part of their lessons, so online safety is important in primary and secondary school. Even if your child doesn't have a smartphone and you always supervise them at home when they are using the computer, their friends may well be showing them or introducing them to things that you would rather they did not see and were not aware of just yet.

The impact of the internet and social networking on children and teenagers is something that schools are increasingly having to deal with.

Parent Zone carried out a survey entitled *The Perfect Generation: Is the internet undermining young people's mental health?*. They interviewed young people and teachers and looked in-depth at the experiences of schools. This was the situation as seen by one school:

> The internet and technology are identified here as factors exacerbating an already worrying situation. This school has seen pupils turn to the internet for affirmation, finding negativity or cruelty instead. They worry about pupils' inability to switch off from technology and desire to stay "in the loop", making them unable to take a break from social drama even when they are in

> their own bedrooms. They feel that their pupils are unable to find a balance between online and offline without reliable adult guidance.
>
> They have dealt with students looking up "dark" content about suicide and self-harm, but have also been troubled by worried young people turning to the internet for answers and coming back with unhelpful self-diagnoses. On the other hand, they have also started signposting some students in need of help to reputable websites, saying that much of the best available support is online. Again, they identify trusted adult guidance as the key in helping young people find helpful resources and avoid negative influences online.

A second school in the survey also reported problems spilling over from social media into the school:

> This school does not blame the internet for pupil mental health, but they do feel their pupils sometimes use social media as a platform to be unkind.
>
> For us, dealing with the aftermath when things go wrong, it's not the internet, it's social media. It's not the apps, it's what they do with them. They're mean to each other, they say mean things.
>
> While this has always been a part of teenage life, with the rise of mobile devices, it's become continuous – their students have lost the ability to disconnect for the night at home.
>
> They also see the internet as something that can validate negative behaviour, making bullying and nastiness seem acceptable because it's common and it's easy to do.
>
> This school sees many parents struggling to enforce boundaries about internet use, making it more difficult for their children to manage online time. When parents do set rules, their children can be inadvertently isolated from their peers. One young male pupil feels he has been excluded by his friend group because he's not allowed to play 18-rated games with them outside of school. Each day they come in and discuss the games, leaving him on his own. It is difficult for well-meaning parents to find a balance between restricting inappropriate behaviour and socially disadvantaging their children.
>
> These issues are also playing out with younger children, to the point where some pupils have "taken a step back" from technology by the time they are older. We heard that in this school, some teens even choose to come off social media because they don't want to deal with the negative side.

The effect of the internet on their pupils varies based on maturity levels, friendship groups and, in their view most importantly, home lives. In their experience, young people who have difficult relationships with their parents or whose parents are not willing to set boundaries about online time are more likely to experience problems.

(Rosen, 2016)

You cannot ban your child or young person from the internet, although you may wish you could! The online world is a huge part of their lives. Many of them are only too well aware of the downsides of social networking, yet they are still prepared to put up with these in order to be able to enjoy the positives.

"Screen time" in itself is not necessarily bad. The internet may be being used to conduct research for homework, to collaborate on school projects, to find information on subjects they are interested in, or to seek support from responsible websites. If a child or young person is socially or geographically isolated, it can help them connect and keep in touch with friends at a distance.

But too much time spent online might mean that children and young people are spending less time interacting with friends face-to-face and enjoying physical activities like games and sport, which are good for their mood and fitness. If they are spending any amount of time online, they do need to learn how to stay safe, both to protect themselves from people who might pose risks of various kinds and to avoid getting into trouble through their own online activities. The more time they spend online, the higher the risk.

Your child or young person may be more able than you to understand and use the technology but not necessarily emotionally mature enough to be able to cope with online risks and online interaction with other people.

There is a well-known disinhibiting effect of being behind a screen – people do and say things that they wouldn't do in person. This can get people into trouble – young people, in particular, are more likely to act impulsively and less likely to anticipate risks. Indeed, some may actively seek out risk for the thrill of it.

Parents need to recognise the risks: exposure to online pornography, hate content, violent and disturbing images and videos, fake news, scams, sexting and live streaming, revenge porn, online grooming, gambling sites, cyberbullying, pro-anorexia and pro-suicide websites. Addiction to online games can be another trap, with some young people spending so long on their screens that it interferes with eating, sleeping, socialising and schoolwork.

Online gaming or social networking into the early hours can leave children and young people feeling unable to "switch off", not getting enough sleep and consequently finding it hard to get to school and concentrate on lessons the next day.

Adopted children and young people who have difficulty forming friendships with their peers may be so keen to have friends that they are indiscriminately accepting of anyone who approaches them online. This can get them into trouble if they begin communicating with people who are out to exploit, bully or cause harm to others. Some end up being blackmailed and sexually exploited by people whom they have met online when they have gone along with their requests because they are keen to please and to make friends.

Sharing nude photos is not endemic among all teenagers, and is most common among those aged 15 and over. However, it is worryingly more prevalent among those who are already vulnerable, for example, those in care. The majority of young people share images without experiencing any negative consequences, but again there are significant increased risks for vulnerable young people (see www.internetmatters.org/about-us/sexting-report-look-at-me).

It can be seen as routine for boys to send intimate images in the hope of receiving one back (with no understanding of the need to ask whether someone wants to receive this image in the first place), and similarly girls are asked to send explicit images of themselves. This can become a school issue if such images are circulated around the school and more widely online. This is effectively bullying and sexual harassment, as well as being illegal. School should help parents deal with this. They should have processes for addressing the bullying and sexual harassment aspects, and undertake wider educational work to stop the sharing. They should also provide support to the young person whose image has been shared. While schools don't have clear powers to confiscate devices, child protection processes may be triggered (that can encompass boy/girlfriends), and potentially including the involvement of police. Since these are illegal images, they can be reported to the major social media platforms, which should remove them, and the Internet Watch Foundation can work to get such images taken off the internet.

Parents have many concerns about their children and young people being online:

- He spends too long on his smartphone/tablet.
- She has been sexting.
- They have shared their personal information on social media.
- He has a social media account but he is under 13.
- My teens are using numerous social media platforms and I am not sure how to keep them safe.
- She has been groomed online.
- He is a cyberbully.
- She is being cyberbullied.
- He has seen porn online.
- She is self-harming.
- He has been radicalised online.
- Other people are posting pictures of my child online without permission.

The Internet Matters website has advice about how to address these, along with information on setting controls, filters and privacy settings, and more.

Keep the lines of communication open (as far as is possible with a young person, although this is rarely easy). Make sure you have two-way communication – if it feels like a lecture, they will zone out. Try to ask and listen as much as you speak. Be genuinely interested in what they are doing – it won't be all bad!

Reassure them that you won't blame them or be cross if bad stuff happens to them online – that way, they will be more likely to tell you or ask for help if they get into difficulties.

It can seem overwhelming, and some parents are tempted to give up and just let their child or young person get on with it, but this is a really important part of parenting. Even if you are not technologically skilled, you can still demonstrate that online safety is a family matter, model how you use technology responsibly, and show your child or young person that you are concerned about what they are doing online and that you want to be "present" in their online life. That means talking with them often about what they and their friends do online – taking an interest and discussing with them some of the difficult issues and things that can happen, and asking how they would deal with them. It means agreeing family rules and boundaries and ensuring that children and young people have information and awareness that will help keep them safe.

There's no doubt that it is a scary time to be a parent, but there is a huge amount of information and advice about how to help your child/young person stay safe online. Educate yourself by reading the advice on these websites, among others. Encourage your child or young person to explore the e-safety sites – most of them have sections suitable for all ages, from very young children to teenagers, with games, quizzes, videos and other relatable information. Look at them together.

Useful websites

- www.childnet.com
- www.internetmatters.org
- www.thinkuknow.co.uk
- www.saferinternet.org.uk
- www.parentzone.org.uk

Key points

- The transition to secondary can be daunting, even for young people who aren't adopted. As with starting primary, prepare your young person as much as you can, including talking about it with her and taking her to visit the school.

- Be aware of the additional challenges, such as new classmates, many more teachers, new subjects, higher expectations, greater noise, etc, all of which are potential triggers for adopted young people.

- Make sure you know the key people, such as the support for learning and guidance teachers, the pastoral leads or form tutor, so that you can arrange to discuss any concerns with them.

- Watch out for peer pressure and bullying, both of which can intensify in adolescents; sadly, adopted young people can seem like an easy target. Ask the school to take action straight away if your child is being bullied.

- Consider the quality and effect of your child or teenager's use of screen time and especially social networking. Talk to her about the use of privacy settings and how to stay safe online.

Conclusion: how adopted young people feel in school

We end this book with the views of adopted children and young people. The information reproduced below is from a group of adopted teenagers taking part in the AT-ID (ADOPTEENS) project in Yorkshire and Humberside (www.adopteens.org.uk). They want their teachers and support staff to know that:

- *We want you to stop making snap judgements about our behaviour, and instead ask us what would help.*
- *We need support rather than punishment; someone to talk to and listen, who can help us deal with our emotions.*
- *We want you to have training from specialists to help you understand why we sometimes get anxious, sad, feel mixed up, empty, confused, angry and lonely.*
- *We want adoption to be out in the open so we feel we can talk about it, rather than feeling ashamed or bottling it up.*
- *We need you to stop the bullying by improving how you tackle it.*
- *We want to learn about fostering and adoption in the same way that we learn about LGBT issues and other cultures and religions.*
- *We want help to meet other adopted teenagers; there are probably others like us in school but we don't know who they are.*

And finally, here are the views of some Scottish adopted young people speaking at a Scottish Parliament event at the beginning of Adoption UK's Equal Chance Campaign, September 2018:

Experiences in primary school

It was a very caring school, where everyone took time to really get to know you. The teachers looked out for me and sometimes talked to me about being adopted – some of the other kids had some funny ideas about adoption, thinking I'd grown up in an orphanage or saying, 'But Susie and Ben aren't your real mum and dad, are they?'

(Rosy, age 12)

Horrible – I was always in trouble and didn't feel safe. I used to kick off to get Mum to come in. The school didn't really take responsibility for supporting me – their default response was to call my mum in. They had no understanding of my underlying issues or reasons behind what was going on.

(Luke, age 19)

Experiences in secondary school

Much better. There was a full learning support team and lots of students needing support, so I didn't stand out. What helped was their "can do" attitude and belief in me. They dealt with things immediately, took responsibility for me and saw themselves as capable of handling my issues.

(Luke, age 19)

I want teachers and pupils to know they don't need to treat me differently from everyone else, but just give me a little bit more support and time… even though I've got foetal alcohol syndrome, I'm just like you really and want the same chances as everyone else. It's the adults who need to change their attitude, because the kids can't really change the way they are; our brains are actually damaged – so if we're struggling, we're not being lazy, we really need some practical help!

(Paula, age 20)

About the teachers who made a difference

I think her persistent belief in me and nudging me along the road when I was standing like a stubborn donkey eventually instilled my own belief in myself.

(Laura, age 27)

I could go and talk to the support for learning teacher if I needed help – she took time to get to know me and I was comfortable to discuss my problems with her. She liked me.

(Luke, age 19)

My two P7 teachers were both great – I always felt they were on my side. They knew I was nervous about going up to High School, so they organised for a few of us to go up to the High School for a special tour.

(Rosy, age 12)

My guidance teacher would listen to me, let me rant and took me seriously. He understood ADHD – and took action if someone was picking on me. He cared about people and had that warm, calm and patient manner – everyone liked him. I felt that he genuinely liked me. And it's about mutual respect isn't it?

(Maxine, age 16)

References

Adoption UK (AUK) reports:

- (2014) *Adopted Children's Experiences of School*
- (2017) *Schools and Exclusions Report*
- (2018) *Bridging the Gap: Giving adopted children an equal chance in school*
- (2019) *Top of the Class: How should we be judging our schools?*

Bentley CB (2013) 'Great expectations: supporting "unrealistic" aspirations for children in care', in Jackson S (ed) *Pathways through Education for Young People in Care*, London: BAAF, pp.45–52

Bombèr LM (2007) *Inside I'm Hurting: Practical strategies for supporting children with attachment difficulties in schools*, Duffield: Worth Publishing

Bradbury A and Roberts-Holmes G (2017) *Grouping in Early Years and Key Stage 1: "A necessary evil"?*, London: UCL Institute of Education, available at: https://bit.ly/3pmxR70

CELCIS (2019) *CECYPF Snap Shot View of First Year Reports Presentation*, available at: https://bit.ly/38Lqall

Coram Life Education (film) part of *The Adoptables' Schools Toolkit*, available at: www.coramlifeeducation.org.uk/adoptables

Donovan S (2016) 'How social worker and teacher combined to turn around my son's education', *Community Care*, 18 May

Education Scotland (2018) *Nurture, Adverse Childhood Experiences and Trauma Informed Practice: Making links between these approaches*, available at: https://bit.ly/38yNFO8

Enquire (2019) *Additional Support for Learning: A guide for parents and carers* (2nd edn), available at: https://bit.ly/2Iikowl

Furnivall J, McKenna M, McFarlane S and Grant E (2012) *Attachment Matters for All: An attachment mapping exercise for children's services in Scotland*, Edinburgh: CELCIS

Fursland E (2013) *Facing Up to Facebook: A survival guide for adoptive families*, London: CoramBAAF

Fursland E (2018) *The Adopter's Handbook on Education: Getting the best for your child*, London: CoramBAAF

Hamilton L and O'Hara P (2011) 'The tyranny of setting (ability grouping): challenges to inclusion in Scottish primary schools', *Teaching and Teacher Education*, 27:4, pp.712–721

Henry L (2015) 'The effects of ability grouping on the learning of children from low income homes: a systematic review', *The STeP Journal Student Teacher Perspectives*, 2:3, pp.70–87

Highland Council (2019) *Deferred and Early Entry to School*, Report by Interim Head of Education to Care, Learning and Housing Committee (Appendix 1), Inverness: Highland Council

Hughes D (2012) *Parenting a Child with Emotional and Behavioural Difficulties*, London: BAAF

John B (2017) 'The big decision', *SEN Magazine*, Sept–Oct, Issue 90, available at: https://issuu.com/senmagazine/docs/sen90-final

Marshall N (2018) 'Focusing on attachment', *SEN Magazine*, 8 January, available at: https://senmagazine.co.uk/home/uncategorised/focussing-on-attachment

McCluskey G, Cole T, Daniels H, Thompson I and Tawell A (2019) 'Exclusion from school in Scotland and across the UK: contrasts and questions', *British Educational Research Journal*, 45:6, pp.1140–1159

McEnaney J (2019) *Revealed: Multi-level teaching widespread across Scottish schools*, available at: https://theferret.scot/multi-level-teaching-schools/

NHS Ayrshire & Arran (2019) *Understanding Fetal Alcohol Spectrum Disorder (FASD): Information for parents and carers*, available at: https://bit.ly/35lwyxx

Nock J (undated) 'In a class of their own', *SEN Magazine*, 30 May, available at: https://bit.ly/2UiPUNm

OECD (Organisation for Economic Co-operation and Development) (2014) *Education Indicators in Focus*, available at: www.oecd.org/edu/skills-beyond-school/

RESOLVE: ASL (2014) *Mediation in Education: A user's guide*, available at: https://bit.ly/3kjTEbN

Rosen R (2016) *"The Perfect Generation": Is the internet undermining young people's mental health?*, Parent Zone, available at: https://bit.ly/32xJePK

Scottish Government (2017a) *Mental Health Strategy: 2017–2027*, Edinburgh: Scottish Government

Scottish Government (2017b) *Policy Update: Delivering Getting It Right For Every Child*, Edinburgh: Scottish Government

Scottish Government (2017c) *Included, Engaged and Involved Part 2: A positive approach to preventing and managing school exclusions*, Edinburgh: Scottish Government

Scottish Government (2018) *Developing a Positive Whole-School Ethos and Culture: Relationships, learning and behaviour*, Edinburgh: Scottish Government

Scottish Government (2019) *Children and Young People's Mental Health Task Force Recommendations*, Edinburgh: Scottish Government

Scottish Government (2020) *Support for Learning: All our children and all their potential, Report of the independent review of the implementation of additional support for learning legislation*, Edinburgh: Scottish Government

Seith E (2016) 'Setting puts Scotland's poor at a disadvantage', *Times Educational Supplement – Scotland,* 16 December

South Lanarkshire Council (2017–20) *Attachment Strategy for Education Resources* (draft), Children's Services Plan, South Lanarkshire Council

Treisman K (2017) *Working with Relational and Developmental Trauma in Children and Adolescents*, Oxford: Routledge

Walter S (2016) 'Early experiences in the neurosequential model in education', in Murgatroyd S and Parsons J (eds) *The Canadian Journal for Teacher Research*, Alberta: Collaborative Media Group

We Are Family (2017) *Unattached to School,* 27 October, available at: https://bit.ly/2lssAKz

Who Cares? Scotland (2018) *Response to Consultation on the Empowering Schools: A consultation on the provisions of the Education (Scotland) Bill*, Edinburgh: Who Cares? Scotland

Useful resources

Information, advice, training and support with education issues for parents and schools

Adoption UK

Adoption UK (AUK) is a national charity and network for adoptive parents, with over 10,000 members and offices in each of the four UK nations. It offers a range of support services for adoptive families, including advice, information, online forums, training and peer support groups around the country. Adoption UK in Scotland also includes FASD Hub Scotland and the Kinship Care Advice Service Scotland. AUK has undertaken research and campaigning around education (see Equal Chance). It also aims to provide all school leaders and teachers with knowledge, practical strategies, access to training, and a network of support through AUK's education membership programme.

TESSA (Therapeutic, Education and Support Services in Adoption) is an early intervention programme run by Adoption UK that helps adoptive parents achieve better outcomes for their children by providing access to a clinical psychologist and peer support. More information is available on the AUK website at www.adoptionuk.org/tessa-in-scotland

Scotland office
Great Michael House
14 Links Place
Edinburgh EH6 7EZ
Tel: 0131 202 3670

www.adoptionuk.org/scotland
www.adoption.scot
@AdoptionUKScotland and @AUK_Schools

Attachment-Aware Schools

A partnership between Bath Spa University, Bath & North East Somerset Council, the National College for Teaching and Leadership and a range of other organisations and individuals. They provide training in England, but their website has some useful resources informed by research and based on evidence from classroom practice.

www.bathspa.ac.uk/projects/attachment-aware-schools

Beacon House

While Beacon House therapeutic services are not available in Scotland, they develop freely available resources to promote knowledge about the repair of trauma and adversity for those who need it in home or work settings.

www.beaconhouse.org.uk/resources

Coram Life Education

Coram Life Education has worked with teachers to develop online primary school teacher resources called SCARF (Safety, Caring, Achievement, Resilience, Friendship) to provide a whole school approach, in line with CfE and GIRFEC to support children's physical and emotional health and well-being.

It has also worked with a peer network of adopted young people aged 13–25 in England, The Adoptables, organised and run by Coram, to produce a Schools' Toolkit to teach pupils about adoption. The free Toolkit includes lesson plans, teachers' guidance, films and activities aimed at the England Key Stages 2 (CfE 2nd level, P5–P7) and 3 (CfE 3rd/4th level, S1-S3).

www.coramlifeeducation.org.uk
@CoramAdoptables

Education Scotland (Foghlam Alba)

The Scottish Government executive agency tasked with supporting quality and improvement in education. It is responsible for the inspection and review of Scottish schools and provides information and resources for professionals and parents. The website parents' area is called Parentzone Scotland.

www.education.gov.scot/education-scotland
www.education.gov.scot/parentzone

Emotion coaching

Emotion coaching is an approach used to support children and young people with their behaviour and mental and emotional well-being. It was developed by Professor John Gottman in the USA and there is research on it from England, the USA and Australia. It emphasises the importance of considering the emotions underlying behaviours "in the moment" before dealing with setting limits and solving problems. The aim is to de-escalate difficult situations, increase children's and young people's understanding of their emotions and support their emotional regulation. It involves five steps in the following order: tuning in, connecting, listening, reflecting, and problem-solving.

It is one of the techniques used by schools that are working towards becoming "attachment-aware".

Some schools have introduced emotion coaching as a peer mentoring programme, with selected older pupils being trained to use it with younger pupils.

For further information, see www.emotioncoaching.co.uk and www.bathspa.ac.uk/projects/attachment-aware-schools

Enquire

The Scottish advice service for additional support for learning. It helps parents and carers understand their children's rights to additional support for learning and how to work in partnership with schools and local authorities to ensure their child gets the support they need. It has a helpline and online enquiry service, a young people's website, and produces free guides and factsheets. The free publication, *The Parents' Guide to Additional Support for Learning,* is an invaluable reference.

Tel: 0345 123 2303
www.enquire.org.uk
www.reach.scot (children and young people's website)

Equal Chance Campaign

Adoption UK (AUK) has carried out a series of surveys of adopted parents and children since 2014 which highlighted significant concerns around education. These clearly showed that the reality for many adopted children is that school and college, far from being safe places of opportunity, are a daily struggle.

Adoption UK published the *Bridging the Gap* report to mark the launch of their Equal Chance campaign in June 2018. The report concluded that there are significant gaps in understanding, empathy and resources that are preventing adopted children from having an equal chance to succeed in education.

The Equal Chance Campaign continues to highlight the reality of the school experience for adopted children and calls on the governments of all four nations of the UK to rethink their education systems. The campaign continues to produce regular reports on different aspects of education based on surveys of adopted families, available at: www.adoptionuk.org/equal-chance-campaign.

Fetal Alcohol Advisory and Support Team (FAAST)

A small team based in NHS Ayrshire & Arran, funded by the Scottish Government. It aims to work with multidisciplinary teams in Health Boards across NHS Scotland to improve access to diagnostic services and clinician confidence. It also produces a range of information resources on FASD.

www.nhsaaa.net/services-a-to-z/fetal-alcohol-spectrum-disorder-fasd

Fostering Attachment Awareness to Generate Understanding in Schools (FAGUS)

A framework for measuring the attainment of goals for children in areas that fall outside the academic curriculum. It is a resource for assessing, monitoring and supporting children's emotional and social development and measuring their progress in these areas. It was developed at Beech Lodge School in Berkshire, a specialist independent school that caters for children who have attachment- and trauma-related difficulties, many of whom are adopted (www.beechlodgeschool.co.uk). Other schools can buy the resource to use with particular children who are having difficulties.

It outlines the developmental processes in a child's social and emotional development across 13 different domains, which include: awareness and understanding of others; self-control; motivation and self-efficacy; and moral development. This allows you to identify at what age level a child is functioning and their strengths and weaknesses across each domain.

Teachers can then focus specific interventions to encourage social and emotional progress and measure the child's success.

www.fagus.org.uk
@FagusResource

FASD Hub Scotland

A support service for all parents and carers of children and young people who were – or are suspected of having been – exposed to alcohol during pregnancy. It is funded by Scottish Government and run by Adoption UK in Scotland. Support services include a helpline, Facebook peer support group, individually tailored support and advocacy, training and a range of online resources.

www.adoptionuk.org/fasd-hub-Scotland

FASD Network UK

A social enterprise providing training, consultancy, advocacy and support for families and professionals in the North East of England, and North and East Yorkshire. Website includes free downloadable resources.

www.fasdnetwork.org

Inner World Work

An online resource centre for parents and carers, offering a collection of free, high quality resources to support parents, carers and children who are trauma-experienced. These include information sheets on *What Survival looks like in Primary School*, *What Survival looks like in Secondary School*, and the *Whole Class Happy Pack* of practical, easy, free, grounding and relaxation ideas for teachers to use to create a safer, happier classroom environment. The campaign is run by a group of parents in West Sussex.

www.innerworldwork.co.uk
@InnerWorldWork

Mediation

Mediation is when a neutral and independent third person (a mediator) helps those involved in a disagreement to come together and agree on the best way forward. It can be helpful to include a neutral person or mediator in school meetings if parents and school are in conflict. If the disagreement is about additional support for learning, local authorities must offer free, independent mediation services to try to resolve the disagreement. RESOLVE:ASL is an independent, free mediation service for parents and carers of children and young people with additional support needs, provided by Children in Scotland.

www.childreninscotland.org.uk/our-work/services/resolve

Mentally Healthy Schools

This website provides information, advice and resources to help primary schools understand and promote all children's mental health and well-being.

www.mentallyhealthyschools.org.uk

National Organisation for FASD (formerly NOFAS-UK)

Provides information, training and resources for people affected by FASD, their parents, carers and professionals. The organisation has some useful resources for teachers and teaching assistants. It will also try to help parents who call with queries about children's education.

www.nationalfasd.org.uk

Nurture groups

Nurture groups are an intervention used with vulnerable and disadvantaged children and young people and those who have social, emotional and behavioural difficulties, for instance, those who are withdrawn or aggressive, have low self-esteem, are disengaged from learning, or who won't stay in the classroom.

They are in-school classes of 6 to 12 children or young people in early years settings or primary or secondary schools. Two teachers run the group, providing warmth, acceptance and nurturing experiences to help remove the barriers to the children's learning and help them develop positive relationships with teachers and peers. There is a lot of emphasis on communication and social learning. As well as regular lessons, activities include emotional literacy sessions, sharing news and eating breakfast together.

Children attend nurture groups often on a part-time basis but remain part of their main class group and usually return full-time to their own class within two to four terms.

Nurture groups are evidence-based, have been used in the UK for 40 years and are also used in other countries, including Canada, New Zealand and Romania. They are now in over 1,500 schools in the UK, with 321 in Scotland. Glasgow, Angus and West Lothian are the local authorities with the most nurture provision. Nurture groups are recognised by Education Scotland as being one approach to developing positive relationships and behaviour, and it has published guidance on incorporating it into school practice (www.education.

Useful resources

gov.scot/improvement/self-evaluation/applying-nurture-as-a-whole-school-approach-a-framework-to-support-self-evaluation).

www.nurtureuk.org
@nurtureuk

Scottish Attachment in Action (SAIA)

Aims to make sure that everyone understands the fundamental importance of attachment relationships throughout life, by providing training and consultancy in attachment and trauma to practitioners, parents and carers, and by providing information through social media, conferences, events, newsletters and educational resources. Membership is open to all.

www.saia.org.uk

Attachment and trauma interventions and training for children, families and schools

Consultancies
Louise Michelle Bombèr
TouchBase
www.touchbase.org.uk
@theyellowkite @TouchBase_UK

Kate Cairns
kca Kate Cairns Associates
www.kca.training
@kcatraining

Nicola Marshall
Braveheart Education
www.bravehearteducation.co.uk
@BraveHeartEdu

Dr Jennifer Nock
www.jennifernocktrainingandconsultancy.com
@jennifernocktrainingandconsultancy

Dr Karen Treisman
Safe Hands and Thinking Minds

www.safehandsthinkingminds.co.uk
@dr_treisman

Further reading

Anonymous (2017) *How my Brain Works*, 8 December, available at: www.allaboutmyuniquelife.wordpress.com

AT-ID (now ADOPTEENS) (project for adopted teenagers 11–18 years old who live in Yorkshire and Humberside), available at: www.adopteens.org.uk

Bath & North East Somerset Council/National College for Teaching and Leadership (2014) *An Introduction to Attachment and the Implications for Learning and Behaviour*, available at: https://bit.ly/2IrXnXE

Bergin C and Bergin D (2009) 'Attachment in the classroom', *Educational Psychology Review*, 21, pp.141–170

Carolyn Blackburn (Routledge)
Developing Inclusive Practice for Young Children with Fetal Alcohol Spectrum Disorders: A framework of knowledge and understanding for the early childhood workforce (2017)
Educating Children and Young People with Fetal Alcohol Spectrum Disorders (2012)

Blogfox14, A. p. w. a. (2017) *Adoption: The bear facts*, available at: https://adoptionthebearfacts.wordpress.com

Louise Michelle Bombèr (Worth Publishing)
Know Me To Teach Me (2020)
What About Me? Inclusive strategies to support pupils with attachment difficulties make it through the school day (2011)
Inside I'm Hurting: Practical strategies for supporting children with attachment difficulties in schools (2007)

Bombèr LM and Hughes DA (2013) *Settling Troubled Pupils to Learn: Why relationships matter in school*, Duffield: Worth Publishing

Brooks R (2019) *The Trauma and Attachment Aware Classroom*, London: Jessica Kingsley Publishers

Brown J and Mather M (2014) *Foetal Alcohol Spectrum Disorders: Parenting a child with an invisible disability*, Createspace Independent Publishing

Catterick M and Curran L (2014) *Understanding Fetal Alcohol Spectrum Disorder: A guide to FASD for parents, carers and professionals*, London: Jessica Kingley Publishers

Fursland E (2018) *The Adopter's Handbook on Education (England): Getting the best for your child*, London: CoramBAAF

Geddes H (2006) *Attachment in the Classroom: The links between children's early experience, emotional well-being and performance in school*, Duffield: Worth Publishing

Hughes DA and Bombèr LM (2009) *Teenagers and Attachment: Helping adolescents engage with life and learning*, Duffield: Worth Publishing

Jackson C (2017) *Working in the NHS: The state of children's services, Lutterworth*, Leicestershire: British Association for Counselling and Psychotherapy

Marshall N (2014) *The Teacher's Introduction to Attachment: Practical essentials for teachers, carers and school support staff*, London: Jessica Kingsley Publishers

Mather M (2018) *Dealing with Foetal Alcohol Spectrum Disorder: A guide for social workers*, London: CoramBAAF

Newby C (2016) *The Newby Tribe*, available at: https://bit.ly/35mP0FT

SB-FASD (29 April 2017) *The Same Child Shines When Seen Through a Different Prism*, FASDLearningWithHope.wordpress.com, available at: https://bit.ly/3lhHh1k

Staff R (2015) *Parenting Adopted Teenagers: Advice for the adolescent years*, London: Jessica Kingsley Publishers

Appendix: The education system: the basics

This appendix provides some basic information about the education system, for those who are new to it all. Much of the information is adapted from Education Scotland and Enquire.

Types of schools

Mainstream schools

Nursery schools
There are public and private nursery schools, and nursery classes attached to some primary schools. Children can attend public nursery schools from the age of three, but private nurseries will accept children earlier than this. Scottish Government currently funds up to 600 hours per year of free provision of early learning and childcare for three to five-year-olds and some two-year-olds – which equates to roughly 16 hours per week in term time. This is due to increase up to 1,140 hours.

Primary schools
Depending on when in the year a child's birthday falls, children will attend primary school for seven years between the ages of five and 12, designated Primary 1 to Primary 7 (P1-7).

Secondary schools
Secondary schools are also known as high schools and academies. They follow on from primary school and offer six years of continuing education from Senior 1 to Senior 6 (S1–S6), although children may leave school at age 16. Post 16 education outside of school may include Colleges of Further Education, Modern Apprenticeships or other forms of training.

Non-mainstream schools

Sometimes, even with additional support, mainstream school is not suitable for some children. There are three main options.

Special school

Special schools often contain specialist support services and facilities, and teachers may have a specialist qualification or experience in teaching children with particularly complex needs. There are local authority-run schools and a number of independent or grant-aided special schools (www.specialneedsguide.co.uk/special-needs-schools-in-scotland – guide to independent special schools in scotland).

Special unit or learning base attached to a mainstream school

These offer some of the services of special schools, but in a mainstream setting. Children may be taught full-time or part-time in the unit, or the unit may provide staff to support the child in the classroom.

Residential school

These are for children with very complex needs who require access to very specialised provision, or where meeting a child's complex needs has a substantial impact on the rest of the family.

Centres of Excellence

There are six national Centres of Excellence, which are schools organised to allow gifted children to maximise their potential: four for music, one for sport and one for dance. They are located within comprehensive schools so that students receive a broad general education whilst receiving additional time for specialist study (see https://education.gov.scot/parentzone/my-school/choosing-a-school/centres-of-excellence).

Private/independent/boarding schools

There is a wide range of private, independent and boarding schools throughout Scotland. These cover all stages of education from nursery through to secondary school. Further information is available from the Scottish Council of Independent Schools (www.scis.org.uk) and Scotland's Boarding Schools (www.scotlandsboardingschools.org.uk).

Learning structure

Curriculum for Excellence

Curriculum for Excellence (CfE) is Scotland's national curriculum for children and young people aged 3–18. It aims to enable every child or young person to be a:

- Successful learner
- Confident individual
- Responsible citizen
- Effective contributor

The curriculum is broken into two main stages:

- Broad General Education – aims to provide a rounded education from the early years until the end of S3;
- Senior Phase – from S4-S6, includes studying for qualifications.

Broad General Education is divided into five curriculum levels (Early, First, Second, Third and Fourth) which describe different stages of learning and progress across eight curriculum areas:

- Expressive arts
- Health and well-being
- Languages
- Mathematics
- Religious and moral education
- Sciences
- Social studies
- Technologies

Literacy, numeracy and health and well-being are recognised as being particularly important – these are regarded as being the responsibility of all staff. In addition, there is emphasis on developing skills for learning, life and work, knowledge and attributes needed for life in the 21st century.

Learning in this phase may often span a number of curriculum areas (for example, a literacy project planned around science and technology might include outdoor learning experiences, research and the use of ICT (information and communications technology)). Children and young people should be given opportunities to show how skills and knowledge can be applied in interesting contexts. This is termed interdisciplinary learning.

The Senior Phase curriculum, from S4 to S6 (around ages 15–18), follows a young person's broad general education. It should be planned as a three-year experience and enable young people to extend and deepen their learning and continue to develop skills for learning, life and work, through qualifications and also personal development opportunities such as work experience, volunteering, etc. It supports young people in moving on to the next stage – whether that is college, university, training or employment.

The National Parent Forum of Scotland produce a series of excellent 'Nutshell' guides on CfE.

Getting it Right for Every Child (GIRFEC)

GIRFEC is the national approach to improving the well-being of children and young people. It extends across all young people's services, not just education. The GIRFEC approach for policy and delivery of young people's services at both national and local level should:

- put the best interests of the child at the heart of decision-making;
- take a holistic approach to the well-being of a child;
- work with children, young people and their families on ways to improve well-being;
- advocate preventative work and early intervention to support children, young people and their families;
- ensure professionals work together in the best interests of the child.

There should be planning for every child. For those who require more concerted processes of support across agencies like education, health and social care, a Child's Plan should be drawn up. Child's Plans are single or multi-agency plans based on an assessment guided by the GIRFEC National Practice Model. Thus, if there is a team around the child comprised of individuals from these different agencies and professions, they should all be using the same GIRFEC structure and terminology.

Teaching in groups

Children are taught within different teaching groups at school. Often in primary schools this is done in mixed-ability groups. In some subjects such as English and maths, children may be put into ability sets, in which those of higher, middle and lower abilities sit and work together. This means that the tasks they are set and support they receive in class meet their needs at the level at which they are currently working. Groups may change throughout the year depending on the topic being taught and your child's and other children's progress within the group.

In a 2017 report (Bradbury and Roberts-Holmes, 2017), it was found that grouping by "ability" or attainment is common in Key Stage 1 (equivalent to P1/P2) in primary schools in England and takes many forms. Despite the research evidence that mixed-ability teaching produces higher attainment overall, these practices continue and teachers have concerns about the negative impact of grouping on children's confidence, self-esteem and aspirations, potentially leading to mental health problems. Similar research in Scotland (Hamilton and O'Hara, 2011; Henry, 2015) had already identified similar concerns and highlighted the negative impact on children from already disadvantaged groups. The Educational Institute for Scotland (EIS), Scotland's largest teaching union, was quoted in 2016 as saying that pupils should be taught in mixed-ability groupings as far as possible, but that the grouping practice persists; partly because it has been the norm for generations and partly due to the resource issue associated with mixed-ability teaching being most successful with smaller class sizes (Seith, 2016).

In secondary schools the system is even more prevalent, often called "banding". This is where pupils are grouped broadly depending on their ability and then taught within these groups for most subjects like history, geography and science; sometimes English and maths are more specifically set.

In the Senior Phase, young people of different ages may be taught together as they are working towards the same qualification. However, there have been some concerns over the practice of multi-level teaching, where learners aiming for different qualifications such as National 5 and Highers are being taught in the same class (McEnaney, 2019).

Additional support needs (ASN)

All children and young people need support to help them learn. The term ASN is used for the support that is additional to, or different from, that received by children or young people of the same age, that some children and young people require to ensure they benefit from education and to help them learn. All looked after children are assumed to have ASN until it has been established otherwise. This "automatic" legal assumption does not continue once a child has been adopted, but many adopted children have some kind of additional support need and find school a difficult place to be.

You or your child's teacher may identify concerns. These might be worries around behaviour, peer relationships, lack of progress or physical needs. As explained throughout this book, emotional or behavioural issues can get in the way of your child's learning and limit their progress. Or it may be because your child has a physical need, and adjustments within the classroom or the use of specialist equipment are required.

Additional support may include:

- a special learning programme, such as for maths;
- a nurture group to support social skills;
- specialist equipment;
- extra support from an assistant;
- small group work;
- someone observing and supporting in class or at play and lunchtime;
- assistance in taking part in classroom activities;
- help communicating with other children;

- support with physical difficulties, such as eating, changing for PE (physical education) or using the toilet.

Parents should be involved in discussions and decisions about their child's learning, and each local authority will have a policy explaining how they identify, plan for and provide support to children who need additional help. You have a right to ask your local authority to assess whether your child has ASN. Advice and information are available for parents and young people from Enquire (see Useful resources) and the Factsheet *Identifying and Assessing your Child's Needs* (www.enquire.org.uk/publications/identifying-assessing).

Included in ASN are children whose education is affected by issues resulting from them being highly able or particularly gifted. They need to be challenged to reach their potential, and be protected from any potential bullying because they stand out from others. Highly able refers to a child working, or having the potential to work, ahead of other children and young people their own age across the whole curriculum or in one or more areas. Particularly gifted usually refers to children who have a talent in an area such as music, sport or dance.

Who's who in the education system?

It helps if you understand the roles and responsibilities of the many different professionals in the education system and who to turn to for particular support or advice. There is a great deal of terminology variation between different local authorities and schools, but there is usually some combination of the following:

- Senior Leadership Team (SL Team), incorporating the Head Teacher, Deputy Head Teacher(s), Principal Teacher(s) and often a Business/Resource Manager. In secondary schools, the SL Team may be extended to include Faculty Heads who lead curricular departments.

- Teachers, who in primary school are responsible for a class and teach a large range of subjects. They are likely to be your first point of contact for your child and they will probably get to know you and your child very well. Some primary schools employ specialist teachers to teach subjects such as PE, modern languages, digital learning or music. In secondary school, the structure is different, and your child will have a large number of teachers with specialist subject knowledge. Some secondary schools only have subject classes and there is no division into classes/forms that meet before the start of lessons in the morning or after lunch. Different schools have different arrangements for parents to make contact so you may be directed to Heads of House, Heads of Year, Tutors, etc.

- Support for learning and pastoral support tend to vary a great deal between different schools and to be more structured in secondary schools. More senior staff may be a Principal Support for Learning Teacher or Learning Support Co-ordinator, with other staff designated as Additional Support for Learning teachers, or pupil support assistants/officers/workers.

- Pastoral support is about promoting pupils' well-being. For example, a school might employ a learning mentor who helps pupils to deal with any individual difficulties or issues that might affect their learning, such as poor attendance, low self-esteem and confidence, behaviour or emotional difficulties, settling into a school, bereavement or problems at home. They may work with a pupil on a one-to-one basis or run small groups around a particular area, such as anger management. Pastoral support may be part of the support for learning team or separate to this.

- Early Learning and Childcare (ELC) is primary schools that have an attached nursery school/class and may have an Early Learning and Childcare Manager with Early Years Officer(s) and Nursery Practitioner(s). They may also have their own pupil support staff.

- Other staff may include Dining Room Supervisors (may be for lunch and breakfast, often still referred to as dinner/breakfast ladies), Playground Supervisors, Office staff/ Secretaries/Administrators, Janitors/Facilities Technicians, School chaplains, School Crossing Guides, Cleaners, etc.

Role of local authorities

Local authorities are responsible for the provision of education. They have a legal duty to ensure that there is "adequate and efficient" provision of school education in their area. Local authority staff/services who have direct contact with parents and/or children include:

- Additional support for learning services support learners, families and schools to overcome barriers to learning. They are often divided into teams such as inclusion support for children with complex needs as a result of autism or trauma, literacy and dyslexia support, visual impairment support, etc.

- Educational psychologists work within local authorities, in partnership with families and other professionals, to help children and young people achieve their full potential. They support schools and the local authority to improve all children's experiences of learning. They use their training in psychology and knowledge of child development to assess difficulties children may be having with their learning. They provide advice and training on how schools might help children to learn and develop. They recommend methods, or develop strategies in partnership with schools, to help a child learn more effectively. Strategies may include teaching approaches, improvements to learning environments, advice on curriculum materials and behaviour support.

- Education welfare officers work with schools, pupils, parents and carers to support regular attendance. They become involved with families when a child is failing to attend school at an expected level or is regularly late. They support families and identify difficulties that need attention.

Learning review and assessment

Education plans

All looked after children in education should have a plan in place for improving their learning experience and attainment. A representative from their school would be expected to attend or at least submit information to review meetings for the child. Any child who has already been assessed as having ASN before they start school should have a plan in place before they start. Terminology varies between local authorities and schools; however, there are three main types of education planning:

- **Personal learning planning (PLP)** – should be done for every child. Manageable and realistic aims and goals should be set for the child that reflect their strengths as well as their needs. The aims and goals should be reviewed, and parents should receive reports, for example, at the end of term and at parents' evenings.

- **Individualised educational programme (IEP)** – is a tailored, individualised plan or programme of support which is expected to last up to a year. Learning targets within the plan are usually of multiple months or termly duration, and the plan is reviewed. This plan may also be known as an additional support plan, or other similar name. Parents should be included in review meetings.

- **Co-ordinated support plan (CSP)** – is a statutory education plan prepared by local authorities to identify, and ensure provision of, services for children and young people with complex or multiple ASN where there is multi-agency involvement. Targets should be limited in number and focus on key priorities of learning. They should be simple, clearly expressed and measurable. There are statutory set time limits and review intervals and requirements for parental consultation and involvement.

The statutory criteria and content for a CSP and IEP can be found in *The Supporting Children's Learning Code of Practice* (3rd edn).[1] General guidance on planning additional support can be found in the Enquire *Parents' Guide* (see Useful resources) and the Factsheet *Planning your Child's Support* (www.enquire.org.uk/publications/planning).

Checking progress

In CfE, each curriculum area is planned using experiences and outcomes. These describe the knowledge, skills, attributes and capabilities of the four capacities that young people are expected to develop. They are assessed in many different ways: set tasks, projects, verbal discussion, homework, tests and exams. Benchmarks set out clear statements about what learners need to know and be able to do to achieve a level across all curriculum areas.

What should I expect my child to be assessed on and when?

During the Broad General Education phase, the expectation for most children is that they will cover the Early Level between the age of three and end of P1, First Level during P2–P4, Second Level during P5–P7, and Third and Fourth Levels during S1–S3.

There are online standardised assessments in reading, writing and numeracy as part of everyday learning and teaching (Scottish National Standardised Assessments) in P1, P4, P7 and S3. These help identify children and young

---

1 Statutory Guidance for the Education (Additional Support for Learning) (Scotland) Act 2004 (as amended)

people's progress by providing diagnostic information to support teachers' professional judgement.

Exams and qualifications

Some secondary schools cover the full range of subjects throughout S1–S3; others have learners gradually reduce their range of subjects before they make their final choices for S4. There will be consultation and discussion with learners and parents about their subject choices and their most suitable qualification routes. The full range of qualifications available are on the SQA website (www.sqa.org.uk) but different schools will offer different combinations of qualifications, such as National Qualifications, SQA vocational qualifications (SVQs), National Certificates and Progressions Awards, SQA Awards, Qualifications for Work, and Core Skills.

The National Qualifications are Nationals (Nats) 1–5, Highers and Advanced Highers. In S4, pupils (age 15/16) will study for Nat 1–5s depending on their attainment level in each subject. Nat 5 is the equivalent of the Standard Grade Credit Level or Intermediate 2 in the previous national qualifications. Nats 1–4 are assessed internally, Nat 5 is assessed internally and by external examination. In S5, pupils can sit more Nat 4 or 5s and progress to Highers, the qualification that gives them access to university. Those who stay on for S6 can do more Highers and/or Advanced Highers. Advanced Highers are equivalent to the first year of study at a Scottish university and can gain access to the second year of a course.

There are a wide range of SQA vocational qualifications based on national standards for nearly all occupations in Scotland, such as forestry, catering and construction.

National Certificates (NCs) and National Progression Awards (NPAs) provide those preparing for work with opportunities to develop skills desirable to employers.

SQA Awards are small, flexible qualifications, suitable for any type of learner. They are designed to address and provide proof of specific skills. Examples of awards include Employability, Safe Road User and Personal Finance.

Qualifications for work include Introduction to Work Place Skills and Certificate of Work Readiness and Core Skills, which are five skills that are key to learning and working in today's world, available at levels 2–6 of the Scottish Credit and Qualifications Framework (SCQF), such as Numeracy and Working with Others.

School policies

National policy is to focus on social and emotional well-being and creating a positive school ethos based on mutual respect and trust, in response to research that this has a more positive impact than more traditional punitive approaches. CfE and GIRFEC both support the development and promotion of positive relationships in school. Schools' policies should reflect this and will usually be available on their websites. Parents should contact their child's school if they have any concern about how school policy is being applied. If children/young people struggle to self-regulate and manage their behaviour, this may be an ASN matter and require more investigation and support. Exclusion is used much less than previously but may still be considered, and this is discussed further in Chapter 6.

There has been much concern over reports on the use of restraint and seclusion in Scottish schools (www.cypcs.org.uk/ufiles/No-Safe-Place.pdf) and new guidance is expected soon. Currently, school staff are not allowed to carry out a body search of a child or young person suspected of carrying an offensive weapon – this can only be carried out by the police. They can ask the pupil to empty their pockets and for permission to look through their personal possessions. If permission is refused, this can only be carried out by the police.

Attendance

If you are having difficulty getting your child to attend school, you should receive support from their school.

If your child has a health problem and is unable to attend for a long period of time, you should receive work or tuition for them from their school.

If you have informed the school of the reason why your child is absent, and the school is satisfied that this is a valid reason, these are recorded as authorised absences. Schools will not normally give a family permission to take pupils out of school for holidays during term-time. This would be recorded as an unauthorised absence. It is up to education authorities to decide what sanctions they will use if there is an unauthorised absence. There is guidance for parents at www.gov.scot/publications/guide-parents-school-attendance. More detail is available in the Scottish Government guidance for education authorities (www.gov.scot/publications/included-engaged-involved-part-1-positive-approach-promotion-management-attendance-scottish-schools).

School uniform and general appearance

Each school decides its own rules about pupils' general appearance, for example, hair style, wearing make-up, tattoos, etc. A school can have a policy on general appearance so long as it is reasonable and does not discriminate on grounds of sex or ethnicity. Similarly, there is no specific law regarding school uniform – it is up to the school so long as the school is not discriminating against children because of ethnicity, sex, sexuality, disability or religion and human rights. The school should provide information on its policy on clothing and uniform. The Education Authority should also provide written information on its general policy on wearing school uniform. As a parent, if you do not want your child to wear the school's preferred uniform, your child cannot be disciplined for not wearing it. However, if your child simply refuses to wear school uniform, their school can discipline them if it thinks that academic or disciplinary problems might be caused by the refusal.

Parental involvement

Parent Council

A school Parent Council is a group of parents selected by all parents in the school to represent their views. Parent Councils have an important role to play in school improvement by working closely with the management team while ensuring that the parental perspective is represented and taken into account. They should try to help create an environment where all parents know that their views matter, and where they feel confident and comfortable putting them forward. They work on behalf of all parents to discuss educational matters that are of importance to all. They do not get involved in individual matters relating to children or staff in the school (see www.connect.scot).

Parent Forum

A school's Parent Forum automatically includes every parent/carer with a child enrolled at the school. Parent Forums are a way for schools to encourage more parents to get involved in school life. They are informal groups where parents can raise issues, be consulted on school policy and give their views. They work closely with the Parent Council in deciding how the council should operate and what issues should be worked on. The National Parent Forum of Scotland works at a national level to ensure that parents play a full and equal role in education, and supports parents to get involved in their child's education (www.npfs.org.uk).

Glossary

There are many acronyms and special terms used in education, which can be hard to get to grips with. Here are some common terms used in this guide.

ACE	Adverse childhood experiences
ADHD	Attention deficit hyperactivity disorder
ASD	Autism spectrum disorder
ASF	Adoption Support Fund (England)
ASL	Additional support for learning
ASLA	Education (Additional Support for Learning) (Scotland) Act 2004 as amended 2009
ASN	Additional support needs
AUK	Adoption UK
CAMHS	Child and Adolescent Mental Health Services
CECYPF	Care Experienced Children and Young People's Fund
CELCIS	Centre for Excellence for Children's Care and Protection
CfE	Curriculum for Excellence
COSLA	Convention of Scottish Local Authorities
CPM	Child planning meeting
CPV	Child to parent violence
CSP	Co-ordinated support plan
CYPA	Children and Young People (Scotland) Act 2014
DDP	Dyadic Developmental Parenting
DHT	Deputy head teacher
EIS	Educational Institute for Scotland

ELC	Early learning and childcare
FAAST	Fetal Alcohol Advisory and Support Team
FAGUS	Fostering Attachment Awareness to Generate Understanding in Schools
FASD	Foetal (also spelt Fetal) Alcohol Spectrum Disorder
GIRFEC	Getting It Right For Every Child
GP	General Practitioner
HT	Head teacher
ICT	Information and communications technology
IEP	Individualised Education Programme
KCASS	Kinship Care Advice Service Scotland
LAC	Looked after child
MVP	Mentors in violence prevention
Nat	National (1–5) qualifications
NC	National certificates
NME	Neurosequential Model in Education
NMT	Neurosequential Model of Therapeutics
NOFAS	National Organisation for FASD
NPA	National progression award
NPFS	National Parent Forum of Scotland
NVR	Non-violent resistance
OECD	Organisation for Economic Co-operation and Development
P1	Primary 1 (P1–7)
PAC-UK	Post Adoption Centre UK
PACE	Playfulness	Acceptance	Curiosity	Empathy	
PAE	Prenatal alcohol exposure

PDA	Pathological demand avoidance
PEF	Pupil Equity Fund
PEP	Personal education plan
PLACE	Playfulness	Love	Acceptance	Curiosity	Empathy	
PLP	Personal learning planning
PRU	Pupil referral unit (England)
PSA	Pupil support assistant
RSHP	Relationships, sexual health and parenthood
S1	Senior 1 (S1–6)
SAAS	Student Awards Agency Scotland
SAIA	Scottish Attachment in Action
SCARF	Safety	Caring	Achievement	Resilience	Friendship	
SCQF	Scottish Credit and Qualifications Framework
SEAL	Social and emotional aspects of learning
SENCO	Special educational needs co-ordinator
SHANARRI	Safe	Healthy	Achieving	Nurtured	Active	Respected	Responsible |Included	(indicators)
SL	Senior leadership
SLT	Support for learning teacher
SQA	Scottish Qualifications Authority
SVQ	SQA vocational qualifications
TA	Teaching assistant (England)
TESSA	Therapeutic, Education and Support Services in Adoption
VSH	Virtual school head
WISE	Walk away	Ignore	Share	Educate	

AdoptionUK

in Scotland
Together we're family

[Ad]option UK is the leading charity for adoptive families, and others [par]enting children who can't live with their birth families, such as kinship [car]ers. Most of today's adopted children have suffered violence, neglect [an]d abuse in their birth families, with lasting impacts on their relationships, [lear]ning and health. We connect families through an active community of [ado]pted people and adopters; provide direct support through therapeutic [ser]vices, advice and training; and campaign to influence government [ad]option policies and adoption practice.

[Ou]r aim is to give children who have had an unfair start [in li]fe an equal chance of a bright future.

CONTACT US

Helpline: 0300 666 0006 • Mon-Fri: 10am-2.30pm
scotland@adoptionuk.org.uk
@AdoptionUKScotland @AUKScot @AUKScot
0131 202 3670
www.adoptionuk.org/scotland • https://adoption.scot/

FASD hub Scotland • Kinship Care Advice service for Scotland • TESSA in Scotland